The Miracle of Intention

DEFINING YOUR SUCCESS

By

Pat Davis

Foreword by
Burke Hedges

Published by
Network Marketing Tutor, Inc.
San Diego, California

Network Marketing TUTOR™

The Miracle of Intention
Defining Your Success
By Pat Davis
Foreword by Burke Hedges

©2000 Network Marketing Tutor, Inc. • San Diego, California • USA

Published by:
Network Marketing Tutor, Inc.
7770 Regents Road #113-207
San Diego, California 92122
Phone (888) 952-7000

Cover design: Tony Giovanni—onlineideas.net

Printed in the United States of America
First Edition November 2000

To my husband and soul mate, Ollie. Thanks for always being by my side for over 40 years. I never thought that I could love you more than I did on the day we were married, but I was wrong. As time goes by, I keep discovering new and wonderful reasons for loving you even more. Thank you for always supporting, encouraging and believing in me. I look forward to our next 40 years together.

Contents

Acknowledgments

Like many books, this one was two years in the making. During that time, the manuscript underwent many changes, as did my life. Without the constant support and encouragement from Uma Outka, my editor, these pages would still be on the computer. Thank you for encouraging me to get it all down, get it right and most importantly to finish it. I certainly could not have done it without you.

Thanks to Burke Hedges and Katherine Glover at INTI Publishing for believing in my message. A warm special thanks to Tony Giovanni for being with me from the early outline days to designing and putting all the finishing touches on my cover. A personal thanks to you, Bev, for coming back into my life and sharing your new self with me. Kevin McCarthy and Brian Biro, you both showed that you are always my friends and true professionals when you graciously and generously shared some of your great materials. Chris Gross, thanks for helping me find the title that expressed the message I wanted to share. Rusty Burrier and Tricia Seymour, your quotes from your *Rise to the Stars: A Daily Focus*

Book for Network Marketing Entrepreneurs, added just the right thought-provoking quotes throughout. Deep appreciation goes to all the successful and busy networkers who took of their time to contribute . . . thanks Steve and Melissa Huszczo, Sandra Tillinghast, Mark Eldridge, Joyce Oliveto and Judy Berg.

I owe a great deal of thanks to all the special people whose sharing and mentoring helped me be who I am today. There are too many of you to mention. If our paths have crossed, I'm sure that in some way you have contributed and I appreciate it. I am especially grateful to two very strong mentors in my life. One is Mulford J. Nobbs (Nobby), the first person that truly taught me to value and respect the direct sales industry. His was the first and only network marketing company that I belonged to, and I stayed for twenty-five years. The second is John Kalench, a training icon in the network marketing industry. I had the privilege of a focused tutelage with John for five years. Both these men shared with me their intense passion and belief in the opportunity of the direct sales and network marketing industry. This passion created the basis from which I grew my network marketing business and continue to grow my Network Marketing Tutor, Inc. business today.

A huge thanks to my children Matthew and Laura. This book contains some of our life's journey together. I am so proud of both of you. I sincerely acknowledge the patience and support you give your entrepreneurial mother. I'm fortunate to have such great children. Our family has grown even more with the addition of your wonderful spouses—Audrey and Mike. Thanks also, Matt and Audrey, for my first grandchild—a beautiful granddaughter, Megan Jewel, whom you named after me. (I am sure more grandchildren will come after the publication of this book, so don't any of you take offense. Nana will catch you in the next printing!)

Last but not least, to all my many friends, thank you for being my friend.

Foreword

As an individual who has sold more than 2 ½ million books on the subject of personal growth, network marketing, and free enterprise, I know a great book when I read one. *The Miracle of Intention* is a great book because it provides the reader with a bulletproof formula for success in network marketing.

Early in the book, Pat Davis asks an important question: Why is it that so many people approach their network marketing business with the hope of achieving their dreams, but end up giving up and justifying why they should settle for a life of mediocrity and complacency? Why is it that so many people start their network marketing business with big hopes and big dreams but fall way short of their expectations?

Pat's answer to these questions? The Miracle of Intention. I couldn't agree more. You see, people who succeed exemplify the miracle of intention. They *intend* to be successful. They don't *wish* to be successful. And, as Pat points out, a person with a strong intention is, by definition, a committed person and therefore, will be a successful person.

Pat Davis has magnificently prepared a recipe—a strategy—for the first-time network marketer and for the experienced professional to follow. *The Miracle of Intention* is filled with stories that will not only entertain, but also will teach the many necessary lessons you must know if you intend to be successful in network marketing. Pat shares the strategies that are proven to command the results you desire. She shares the message of hope that you *can* live your dreams, and she asks thought provoking questions that stimulate and motivate the miracle of intention.

If you are ready to turn your life around and begin the pursuit of your dreams, this is the book for you. If you are ready to integrate the miracle of intention into your life, you *will* have more . . . do more . . . and be more.

Burke Hedges
Author
You, Inc., Discover the CEO Within
Who Stole the American Dream?
You Can't Steal Second With Your Foot on First!
Read and Grow Rich
DreamBiz.com
Copy Cat Marketing

Introduction

Congratulations! If you're picking up this book, you've probably made the wise decision to start a network marketing business. As someone who's been in this industry for more than 29 years (I tell everyone that I started in kindergarden!), I can say without a shadow of a doubt—it's a great choice.

If you're like most people, life for you (and probably most of the people you know) is busier than ever. For so many American families, money is tight, time is tight, and there doesn't seem to be any way out. Someone told *you* about network marketing, and fortunately you had the clarity of mind to see this rare opportunity for what it really is—incredible.

I wrote this book for a couple of reasons.

First, I love network marketing and want to convey to as many people as possible what I know to be true—that this business lets you pursue success by *your* definition. There are testimonies of ordinary people earning millions for their work in network marketing and of many more who may not be millionaires, but are earning more than enough to make a significant positive difference in their life. There are a lot of benefits besides income to be gained by simply being involved in this industry, but since money tends to be the measuring stick we use for evaluating success, it is usually the focus.

I greatly value the fact that earning potential is directly proportional to effort in this rare business, but it's the personal growth that network marketing makes possible which truly excites me. This unique industry allows individuals from all different backgrounds to make *meaningful changes for the better* in their lives. With this book, I want to communicate what a gift it is to have a vehicle for achieving and defining *your* success. This business is about the choice to pursue what will make a lasting difference in *your* life. The choices we make will all be different, and that diversity is one we should be proud of and take joy in.

Second, far too many people get started in network marketing but then don't stick with it long enough to see the things they came in hoping to see materialize. Regretfully, they don't make it to payday. This happens for a variety of reasons. Sometimes it's because they never took the time to find out what *they* wanted and are pursuing a dream that rings hollow; sometimes it's that their goals were bigger than their commitment, making them more like wishes that quickly came to seem unattainable; sometimes it's that they never really believed in themselves or in network marketing, and their meaningful goals became victims of doubt.

The aim of this book is to change that pattern and help as many people as possible actually attain what they came to the business for—whatever that may be—and possibly even more.

Four key points you will learn in this book are:

- **You define your success.**
- **That definition will evolve.**
- **Begin where you are.**
- **Your own true intention is the answer.**

I believe very strongly that whatever you started your network marketing business to achieve, you *can*—through the miracle of your own intention to do so. Intention is such a vital and often misunderstood part of success. When you truly intend to do something, you do it. When you hear people say things like, "I intended to, but . . ." the truth is that they didn't intend to *really*. The true intention was more likely to do whatever it was if it felt convenient, or if they were in the mood, or it was easy enough. Understanding how powerful your intention is and learning how to leverage it will ensure your success in this business. It requires real work and persistence—and the rewards are worth it!

Pat Davis
San Diego, CA

SECTION ONE

Define Your Success

Define Your Success

After grabbing a quick bite to eat at her favorite bistro, Andrea checks her makeup in a pocket mirror, pays the tab (leaving a generous tip), and walks briskly out to her car. She's in a good mood today. Last week an associate showed her The Greatest Company Ever's compensation plan, and her jaw about dropped to the floor. As a stockbroker with a large firm, she knows numbers, and it didn't take her long to realize that this company could be her ticket out of the 12-hours-a-day corporate rat race. She promptly ordered a sample of every product and marketing tool the company offers, and tonight, she's on her way to her first meeting—prepared with a full page of questions to ask the most successful person there. She's confident that she'll make it to the top pretty quickly—she has in every other endeavor, and she won't let this be any different.

•••

Elizabeth has spent all day reading through her starter kit—she just signed up with The Greatest Company Ever three days ago. She gets a little dressed up, and after going over dinner instructions with the baby-sitter and kissing her two kids good-bye, she heads out to the car carrying her purse and her brand new business planner. This is her first meeting, and she feels a rising excitement—the idea that she might be able to replace her $24,000-a-year administrative assistant salary with a network marketing income from home. She had no idea this was even possible. She sings along to the upbeat music on the radio as she drives.

•••

David enrolled in The Greatest Company Ever four months ago to buy products wholesale. He tried them when a friend saw how exhausted he had become while getting his computer consulting business off the ground. His friend told him that the products would make him feel more energetic. As it turned out, they did! Tonight, David has decided to attend the local meeting. He's been thinking that just maybe this could be another little income stream—already his mom and brother have started using the products, too. His love is computers, but you never can have too many irons in the fire, right? And he's been interested in nutrition ever since his year in the Peace Corps after college, when he helped bring malnourished children back to health. As he drives to the meeting, his mind is open and he's curious to see if the business might be a fit for him. . . .

•••

David, Elizabeth, and Andrea all arrive at the hotel around the same time—a few minutes before eight o'clock—walk in, and follow the signs to the conference room. The room is filling up with people. Elizabeth sees her sponsor across the room, her cousin, Mike, who's already reached the first level in the company. He has brought a few others who are considering the business and introduces them to her.

David finds a spot near the back of the room to stand and observe what's going on. Andrea walks up to the couple at the front of the room—it's clear they will be giving the presentation—and introduces herself before taking a seat in the front row.

As the people sit down, the couple at the front gets the group's attention. "Good evening, everyone! I'm Jim, and this is my wife, Betty. We're Diamond Executives with The Greatest Company Ever, and we're here to tell you that you can achieve your wildest dreams with this company. This is the best possible time to get involved, and we're going to help every single one of you in this room who is willing to earn a six-figure income with the plan we're about to teach. Is that something you'd like to learn about? We thought so—let's get started. . . ."

•••

When the presentation ends an hour later, Andrea stays on for another half hour going over her questions with Jim and Betty. Everything she's heard tonight confirms what she thought—this *is* a business that will let her meet her financial goals with a lot more freedom than she has at the brokerage firm. Jim and Betty couldn't be more pleased to provide answers.

Saying something about relieving the baby-sitter, Elizabeth waves good-bye to Mike over the shoulders of his guests, gathers her things, and makes her way back to her car. She gets in and sits back for a moment before turning the key in the ignition. She feels overwhelmed and, for some reason, a little depressed. The excitement she felt on her way to the meeting is gone, and she leaves the radio off as she drives home, thinking, "I'm not sure I can do this after all. . . ."

David grabs a drink at the water fountain on his way out, gets in his car, and heads straight home. He feels a little turned off—all that focus on money. It's clear they just want more commitment than he's willing to give, considering he's already got a business of his own that he's happy with. "Oh well," he says to himself, "I have enough to do as it is without taking on something else." He doesn't regret going to the meeting and he'll continue as a wholesale customer, but the business just isn't for him.

•••

This scenario demonstrates an all-too-common occurrence in network marketing. People get involved for many different reasons—their own reasons—and what's so unique about the business is that it can fill just about any need. But how many people drift away after their initial excitement is dampened, not realizing how much choice there is for the taking?

Network marketing is unendingly versatile—it can serve many, many purposes. Some people are simply interested in a company's products; others choose this business in order to be home with young children; replace the income from a high-stress job; get out of debt; pay for education; generate some disposable income; get a new car (like me!); fire their boss; fund the realization of a lifelong dream; or even just make enough more per month to create financial peace of mind. I think I love this aspect of the opportunity the most—the fact that it lets each of us pursue and achieve what we want individually. Success may mean one thing for you and something utterly different for the next person you sponsor, yet the business can support both equally.

The problem is that sponsors sometimes, however unknowingly, impose their own definitions onto those they enroll. In the scenario we just witnessed, that was exactly what happened. The presenters, Jim and Betty, loved network marketing particularly for its incredible income potential. That meant the most to them, and for Andrea, it was a perfect presentation because it meant the most to her too. Maybe your goal is to become a millionaire. If it is, more power to you; it's been done many times in this industry. However, in network marketing, as with any industry, there will always be a smaller number who are willing to do all that is necessary to reach the top of their chosen field. The well-known 80/20 rule applies to the top dollars earned in network marketing—the top 20 percent of the people make the top 80 percent of the income.

Unlike in other industries, however, the good news here is that the remaining 80 percent majority can still benefit greatly from the opportunity. That's what was missing in the presentation, and what led Elizabeth and David to incorrectly assume that the business doesn't offer what they came for—that since "big money" wasn't their goal at the time, network marketing probably was just not for them. What a loss this is for people like them—Elizabeth will continue in the job she doesn't love, and David will give up the chance to build a second income stream to complement his consulting business.

It's also a loss to the industry itself when people like them drift away. Many go on to spread false and negative information about it based on the sour feeling that comes with giving up on dreams. Even more importantly, it takes people of all kinds and with all different goals to make the industry flourish, and you never know— if they'd stayed involved, their definitions of success may have grown and driven them to be top leaders in the field.

My Story

One of the best ways I know of to explain what I mean by the notion of "success evolving" is to share my own networking story. When I meet people, I always want to know the scoop on them, and I'm sure you're wanting to know the scoop on me. Just who is Pat Davis, and what makes her so ecstatic about the rewards of network marketing?

I started in network marketing more than 28 years ago. One of my best girlfriends, Frances, invited me to an "in-the-home" party. I vividly remember saying to Frances, "I just don't go to these in-the-home parties, so no thank you, I'm not going to come." But she kept pestering me about it, saying, "Pat, this woman is coming, and I promised to have at least six people there. You can at least be a body, you don't have to buy anything, I just really need you to be there."

You have to understand that Frances was the kind of girlfriend who, if I didn't agree, would never leave me alone. I decided it was easier to go than have to deal with her later, so I committed to attend with the understanding that I would not make any purchases. With that attitude, and also very little knowledge about how the industry worked, I most certainly didn't go to this in-the-home demonstration to make a career change.

Like many young couples, my husband Ollie and I had just

bought our first home and were really struggling financially at the time. As was typical for a couple our age, we didn't have any furniture in the living room and were still adjusting to the mortgage payments, so there was no way I could spend anything on these frivolous in-the-home parties. But I went and ended up buying $40 worth of products; to put that in perspective, my mortgage payment was $90 (no, I didn't live in a one-room shack, it was the price of a mortgage payment in 1971). Looking back, that was quite a substantial amount to purchase, especially after I said I wouldn't buy anything. It was almost equal to half of my mortgage payment. If I bought half of my mortgage payment today, I would be someone's favorite client.

The next day, Frances called me and asked if I would host a party at my house. I reminded her that I rarely went to such parties and in no way would I agree to host one. In the end, though, I booked one for her because again, it was easier to book a party than deal with her later. Already more involved in the situation than I'd ever expected to be, lo and behold, about two days later, knock-knock at the door and there stands Frances and her husband Gerald, my husband's best friend. In fact, Ollie had been best man in their wedding, and Gerald had been best man at our wedding. Here were our long-time dear friends standing at the door, and all I could think about was that it was dinnertime. I thought, "Why are they showing up for dinner?"

Well, before I could even mention eating, our friends said, "We are so excited—we have this great opportunity for you."

"Stop right there, Frances. You don't understand," I said. "I came to your party, I bought more than I intended at your party, I booked a party. Three out of four! Please leave me alone."

She quickly answered, "But they give cars."

She'd finally hit my hot button, and I wanted to hear a little more. At that time in our lives, we had only one car. For those of you who remember what it was like in the early 1970s, having two cars was a luxury, not a necessity like it is today. For me to keep the car during the day as a young mom and housewife, I had to take Ollie to work in the morning and go back to pick him up in the evening. Something always seemed to come up, like one of the kids wanting to nap when it was time to go get him. When you have babies to pack up and take along with you, it can be a big production. To have a second car would have been incredible—the life of luxury to me. The prospect of a new car of my very own was completely exciting.

There were two problems, though. First of all, the business was a custom-fitted bra business, and I couldn't even begin to imagine going out and selling bras. I was very modest, very shy, and conservative. So even though I wanted to believe that this opportunity could provide me that second car, I had my first doubt: Could I really sell this unusual product that required me to fit other women? I really doubted I could do that. Maybe the car wasn't such a good idea.

My second doubt came quickly as well. To get started, I had to buy a $500 bra kit, and I didn't have $500. But I really wanted the car, so I decided to push that doubt aside for the moment. I went to observe another party, only this time looking at it as a business. When I saw all of the women buying, I decided it could be lucrative for me. I wanted to start my own business, but the $500 initial investment might as well have been $50,000. I just didn't have the money. I actually went to three banks to borrow the money and was turned down all three times, but I just couldn't get my mind off that car, so I pushed forward and applied to a fourth bank. Finally, I found a banker who agreed to lend it to me. I've always wondered if it was because I looked so pitiful by that time, or because he couldn't turn down a small-busted woman who needed $500 worth of bras.

With all the paperwork signed and the check in the mail, the opportunity to create some cash flow was a reality. I remember one of the other distributors lending me her bra kit for a few hours while I was waiting for mine to arrive. I remember to this day running around up until midnight, going to cousins' and friends' houses, I was so enthusiastic. You have to understand, my husband was working very hard—50-to-60 hours a week—but the paycheck he got on Friday barely took us to Wednesday. I hear people saying that they live week to week, but at that time I'd have thought making it all the way from Friday to Friday would be real progress and a level of success. That's just where we were in life.

Even though Ollie worked a lot of hours, he agreed to baby-sit our daughter Laura, who was four years old, and our son Matthew, who was nine years old, twice a week in the evening. He was very firm, though, that two nights a week was the maximum he intended to baby-sit. After my first party, I came home with all the money from the sales and quickly sorted it into two piles: one for my cost of product and what would have to be sent into the company, and one that I thought was probably my profit. Ollie came into the kitchen and saw me doing the "accounting" for my new business. He looked at one pile and said, "So you sold $50?" and I proudly said, "No, I think this is mine." The next night, the same thing happened, except my profit pile totaled $80. Now that may not seem like much by today's standards, but in the 70s, $25 to $40 an hour part-time for a young mom was good. Come to think of it, I bet there are be some young moms today who could get excited about that for part-time earnings.

On the third night, as I was sitting there on the sofa watching TV with Ollie, he asked, "What are you doing home?" I said, "I did my two parties for the week just like we agreed to." "Well," he quickly said, "if you want to do more, you can." He saw the money right away. You see, with just that $130, I'd made a significant difference in our weekly income in just two nights through network marketing. His support was all I needed to be off and running in my new business. I had no experience in sales or management, or even many of the skills you'd think would be necessary to eventually build a multi-million-dollar business and be the U.S. vice president of a $300 million worldwide company (just a peek into where the future took me).

I was fortunate that both Frances and I—she was as green as I was—were sponsored by an upline who was even more passionate about the opportunity we had to offer than the product. This upline instilled an early appreciation in me for the benefits of sharing the opportunity. Her name is Beverley Toney-Walter, and we are still friends today, 29 years later. Bev helped me realize quickly that if I shared the opportunity, I could really increase my income. With that information, the gate was open and I was gone. I was like the bumblebee you studied in science—its body is much too heavy to fly in comparison with its wings, but it flies anyway. Many believe it flies simply because it doesn't know it can't. Well, I was like that bumblebee. I sold and recruited quickly and didn't have enough fear and doubt to realize I couldn't. My intention was to earn a car—and fast.

Network marketing changed everything for me, and a few months later, I'd earned the car that I had dreamed of in the beginning. I'll never forget when a friend took me to the dealership to pick up my brand new Mercury Montego (if you remember this discontinued model, congratulations, you are old enough to buy beer!). Today I would think of it as a gaudy bright gold. However, back then to me, it was the most gorgeous car I had ever seen. When Ollie came home from work that night, he asked, "Where did you get the car?" "It's my company car," I said. "I told you I was going to get the car, and I got the car." From that moment on, I always drove a brand new car completely paid for, including taxes and insurance, from my network marketing efforts (and in case you are wondering, yes, the models and colors of my cars did improve).

From the early days I've been describing, when my definition of success was simply a new car of my own and a little extra spending money, I went on to build one of my company's largest organizations in the United States, with my group producing multi-million-dollars in volume. After 12 years of building in the field, I joined the corporate staff and became vice president of sales for the U.S. This is not necessarily a transition I would recommend, but at the time it seemed like the right decision for me. In hindsight, it served to make me who I am today and provided me with a whole different view of the industry from the corporate side. I worked in that corporate position for 13 years, making it a total of 25 years with the same network marketing company.

In 1994, I felt the time was right to redefine success for myself yet again and became a part of Millionaires in Motion, Inc., in San Diego, California. This independent training company was founded by the internationally known author and master trainer

John Kalench. John acknowledged my love and passion for network marketing and welcomed me to join him in his love of training and educating people in, as John said, our "glorious industry." I feel fortunate to have had the opportunity to have been mentored by John, and my time with his company also offered me an opportunity to make a difference to even more networkers worldwide.

After serving four years as Millionaires in Motion, Inc.'s CEO, I resigned in December 1999 with the intention of achieving my next goal—owning my own training and consulting company serving the direct sales and network marketing industry. This company, Network Marketing Tutor, Inc., is something I could never have imagined when I first started my journey in this industry. But as with any journey, new doors can open up to us that would not have if we hadn't taken those first steps. The most exciting thing about success to me is how it can change and be redefined. A lot of times we don't even realize what life lessons we are learning or what mountains of success we are climbing until we look back.

In my own case, the money is the most visible thing, but upon deeper reflection, I see the incredible impact this business had on my family and the ways in which I developed as a person. I experienced my first airplane trip attending a national convention. I found out what it felt like to stay in five-star hotels. My whole family learned how to dine and not just "eat out." We enjoyed great family vacations from Caribbean cruises to Europe. I gained self-confidence, made life-long friends, and paid for my children's college education. Even Ollie was able to go back to college at age 40 and get his degree. And the very best part was that I was able to share the opportunity to define and achieve success with others as well.

If you're still wavering over whether or not to put forth a real effort in this business, I hope you have a friend like Frances in your life who will drag you along for a while if that's what it takes. I hope he or she will persist as Frances did with me until you make a commitment, because this person you may be considering an aggravating friend is really a rare *true* friend. Then you need to be a persistent friend, a "Frances" for others—helping them to push forward and achieve the things that will change their lives for the better.

What Do You Want Out of Network Marketing?

For now, put aside any doubts you've been feeling and contemplate the following questions:

What is one thing that, if it were different in your life right now, would contribute to your happiness?

_____

_____

_____

_____

What could you have in your life that would make you excited about getting up every morning?

_____

_____

_____

_____

What was the first possibility that came into your head when you understood what your sponsor was explaining about network marketing?

_____

_____

_____

_____

What have you been wanting to do for a while now, but haven't been able to afford the time or money for?

_____

_____

_____

_____

If you are usually worried about not having enough money, what additional amount in your bank account every month would allow you to reduce the stress in your life and relax?

_____

_____

_____

_____

Answering these questions is the first step in the process of identifying your own reason for being attracted to the network marketing industry—defining what I call your "wanna." Gaining clarity about what rewards you want for your efforts in this business is critical to your success.

What is it that you want from this business?

What is your goal—your "wanna"—today? This isn't about what you think you *should* want or what someone *else* wants for you, but what you want deep in your heart for *yourself.*

The reason this is so important is because it's a clear definition of success that sparks the miracle of intention. Why do I use the word "miracle"? Because when you have a strong and clear intention to see something take place in your life, *even if you have no idea at first how it will come to be, it will.* Be aware that an intention and a wish have nothing to do with one another. As an everyday example, you can *wish* you weighed 30 pounds less, but unless it becomes your *intention* to lose the weight, nothing will change. Consider the difference in the level of commitment in these two statements: "I wish I could lose weight," and "I intend to lose weight."

See the difference? A wish is out of touch with what it takes to make it real. A wish to lose weight is not the same as an intention to exercise or eat better.

On the other hand, the necessary actions are implicit in a genuine *intention* to lose weight. The same applies in this business. You can *wish* to replace your current salary with network marketing income and never pick up the phone once, but if you *intend* to replace that salary through your business, you'll be getting in as many calls each day as you can. A person with a strong intention is, by definition, a committed person. This is reflected in the smallest, simplest things we do in life. You intend to show up for work so it doesn't even occur to you not to—you're committed to a level of performance and not being fired, so you make it happen. If you intend to take a vacation, you make reservations and figure out later how to get everything done before you leave. And you show up at the right time to get on the plane.

This is what is so miraculous about intention. A genuine intention *always* yields the intended results.

Revisiting Your Goals

Please don't take goal-setting lightly—and don't let those you bring into the business take it lightly either. Goals form your foundation of strength as doubts or challenges arise during your journey to success. Be very honest about which of your goals are intentions and which are wishes. Spend time defining what success means to you, and as time goes on, allow that definition to evolve. If someone had told me to set a goal of becoming a multi-million-dollar producer in my company, I would have laughed at the preposterous suggestion; success evolves, you just can't always predict how. So having a strong, grounded reason for why you are in the business *now* is a critical part of the foundation from which you'll be able to grow and evolve over time. With it firmly and distinctly identified, the doubtful moments will be few, and if they do creep in, they will be very brief and disappear quickly in the face of your clarity.

If you have been in network marketing for some time and are not achieving all that you want, revisit this. You may have thought you were grounded in your "wanna," but upon reflecting honestly with yourself, you may discover that it could use strengthening. If you don't have a strong reason for being in the business—one that you're excited about—clearly in the forefront of your mind, it won't matter how much training you receive or how many meetings you attend, the moments of doubt will show up, drag you down, and threaten to stop you in your tracks. Your intention to succeed will shift to an intention to avoid challenging situations.

If people in your downline are struggling, explain this to them and help them revisit their goals too. This is critical not only to your personal business but also to everyone else you sponsor. One of the very first essential things to do with a new distributor is take the time to help them understand this concept and clearly define their "wanna." I believe this is more important than any training you may think they need. If you thoroughly train them on product, the company, prospecting methods, etc., but neglect to work with them on their strong reasons for doing the business, they will most likely just sit at home being educated non-achievers. Their life span in the business will be shortened as well. Get them connected to their "why" strongly enough in the beginning and they will have the strength to push forward. We not only want to sponsor and share our opportunity with others, we want them to stay in the business—retention is directly tied to this principle.

When she heard I was writing this book, Judy Berg—a successful networker and friend of mine—wrote me about an exercise she learned in a company leadership training that helped her to understand the importance of intention. I share with you here what she shared with me because it's a great way to understand the way "why" relates to "how" in any endeavor you pursue:

Dear Pat,

I love the title of your book and this is why. . . . [My company's leadership] training contains an exercise in which people are asked to assign "relative" percentages to the following formula:

Intention + Mechanism = Results

What percentage of your results comes from intention versus mechanism—your means or vehicle for achieving them? The correct response is that intention must be 100 percent and mechanism 0 percent. Why? It's back to the familiar adage "where there's a will, there's a way." If you are not 100 percent committed (*intention*), you will never get the results you want—there will always be an excuse or another priority.

This creates some debate because people think there needs to be a figure to represent that a mechanism *does* exist and is necessary—however, we are talking about relative importance, and intention is everything. People rarely fail if they are 100 percent committed to seeing what they want become reality. They may have to try different mechanisms and perhaps find along the way that some don't work, but if they have 100 percent intention, they achieve their goals.

An exercise that gave us a visual understanding of this point involved all participants lining up on one end of the room. Each participant is told that he or she must get to the other side of the room but cannot use a means of getting there that has been used by anyone else. People hop, dance, skip, crawl, etc. What the exercise shows is that if you choose to get there, you will find a way. Even if your original mechanism is taken away, your creativity will kick in because you have the intention of crossing the room. Everyone always finds a unique way to complete the exercise no matter how many people have gone before and taken away the means they thought they had available to them.

I think our current economy can best be described like the frog you attempt to put into hot water. He will resist and jump out. But, if you put a frog into cold water and gradually turn up the heat, he will slowly and comfortably succumb to the warming water and eventually perish. We have succumbed to the "jobs mentality" which all too often robs people of their personal drive, innovation, and excitement. It has taken away the creativity and resourcefulness which we've historically relied upon to create our own destiny. What a waste of human potential!

Today, I know I can be part of changing the model of the economy for the better. It will be one in which people can dream, grow, and flourish and choose to be the best they were intended to be. Through network marketing, I play a part in helping people reach their full potential, by freeing them to help themselves. Never have I felt more positive about the future, for our society, for my family, and for me.

Warm Regards,
Judy Berg

What Judy learned in the training is most powerfully expressed by Brian Klemmer, a speaker and author of the book *If How To's Were Enough We'd All Be Skinny, Rich, and Happy.* His book will help you further explore this topic of intention as it relates to results.

Choices

Although defining what success means and developing strong intentions is something all of us can and *should* be doing, it isn't something we're used to doing. I've found that most people will spend more time creating their grocery list than their life list. They don't understand that they have choices in life, that they can do something to make life better.

I'll never forget one instance when I was facilitating a typical goal-setting segment in a workshop. After explaining to the group the importance of goals, I assigned a time for them to reflect and write their goals down on paper. As always, I encouraged them to set both immediate goals and some long-term goals—to think about things that seem reachable now as well as big, down-the-road ideas that may seem beyond possibility right now. I wanted to see how far they could imagine. Then I gave the entire class time to design their future and write their goals in the workbook. I consider this an important and serious exercise, so I always give plenty of time for the students to complete it as it's critical to their growth.

Since my workshops are attended by a wide variety of people from many different backgrounds and success levels, I like to walk around the room and get a feel for how each student is progressing with the exercise. If a student is "stuck," sometimes all it takes is a little dialogue to help them get "unstuck." I am very patient with them, as I realize that many people either haven't been accustomed to, or haven't been taught, this simple goal-setting concept.

As I was walking around the room, I came across a young woman who was just staring into space—she was obviously mentally somewhere else. I thought to myself, "She must be defining her goals very well, she is thinking hard about them. I can't wait to hear about the big goals she has."

So as not to disturb what I thought was deep concentration, I moved on to another part of the room. After about 15 minutes, the time for the exercise was wrapping up. I walked past this young woman again. She still hadn't written a single thing, not one goal in her notebook. I was about to ask if she had any questions when I noticed that she had tears in her eyes. Well, as a workshop facilitator, I have found that you never can tell what could have happened when you weren't looking. All kinds of thoughts were running through my mind.

I stopped and asked, "Is there anything wrong? Why haven't you written any goals?" She looked up at me with tears running down her checks and said, "I haven't written anything because I didn't know I had choices."

She didn't know she had choices . . . didn't know that she had choices in how her life could be . . . didn't know about goal-setting or that there was an opportunity, an industry, that could allow her to not only set goals, but also achieve them.

Not only did she doubt her abilities, she also doubted that there was anything or any path for her to take that could make a difference in the direction of her life. Later, I discovered that she had a very troubled home life, a struggling marriage, a sick child, as well as financial challenges. She had joined her chosen network marketing company mainly because she loved the products, but now it was as if someone had given her a key that unlocked a door she had no idea she could ever go through. She was so overwhelmed with emotion as she visualized what lay on the other side, she could not even put pen to paper.

"I didn't know I had choices"—that response rings in my head today when I think of what wonderful choices network marketing offers to so many people. No matter what that choice is, the lesson is that our business facilitates the choices we all have as individuals. It was only in realizing she really *did* have choices that she was able to form a meaningful intention. I cannot help but strengthen my belief even more in the opportunity of network marketing every time I reflect on that young lady. As the saying goes, "Life is like a canoe—it can turn around quickly." It's never too late to make a change. I hope you remember this story and know that *you* have choices and they are *yours* to make.

Following is an exercise that will help you choose what matters most to you now and define your success. . . .

The Tournaments

This wonderful exercise is the brainchild of my friend Kevin McCarthy, author of *The On-Purpose Person*—a book I highly recommend. To begin with, take out a pad of paper and at the top of separate sheets, write one of the following categories:

- Physical/Health/Recreation
- Financial/Material
- Family
- Vocational/Career
- Social/Community
- Spiritual
- Mental/Intellectual
- Other

Kevin calls these "life accounts," each representing an important aspect of our lives, and you're about to embark on the creation of a "want list" for each. Sit down and do some serious thinking about what you want in each of these areas of life and write down everything that comes to mind. You may find that you have many, many things listed in one category and only a few in another, but that's fine—just be sure to complete the exercise for all eight.

The next step in the exercise depends on our understanding that every want on our want lists *competes* for our resources, time, energy, and talent. We all know that familiar feeling of being "pulled" in many different directions at once. What you're going to do now is use a simple system for discerning what's *really* a priority. That way you can be free to let go of less important wants and commit yourself to the more important ones. This simple system is what Kevin calls "tournaments," and you're going to have two— one for "qualifiers," the second for "the main draw."

Begin by sketching out the following draw-sheet diagram—the

same sort of draw-sheet used for all kinds of competitions like tennis, spelling bees, or Super Bowl playoffs:

FINANCIAL

Quarter-finals	Semi-finals	Finals

1

2

3

4

5

6

7

8

Core
Want

For the "qualifier tournament," pull out your want list for the first category, and in the numbered spaces, list each want sequentially. Consider the wants in spaces 1 and 2 and choose which is more important; advance the one you choose to "round two." Do the same with spaces 3 and 4; 5 and 6, and so on. Make the decisions in pairs for however many wants you listed. If you don't have an even number of wants, simply advance the leftover want to the next round.

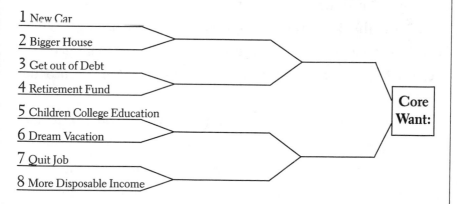

1 New Car

2 Bigger House

3 Get out of Debt

4 Retirement Fund

5 Children College Education

6 Dream Vacation

7 Quit Job

8 More Disposable Income

Core
Want:

The "competition" continues in round two, though now it may be 1 against 4, 6 against 8. Advance the ones that are most important to round three, and then choose between them to identify your top priority in that area of life.

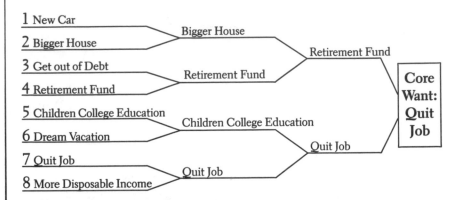

1 New Car
2 Bigger House → Bigger House
3 Get out of Debt
4 Retirement Fund → Retirement Fund → Retirement Fund
5 Children College Education → Children College Education
6 Dream Vacation
7 Quit Job → Quit Job → Quit Job
8 More Disposable Income

Core Want: Quit Job

"But wait a minute," people often object at this point, "I spent lots of time writing out my want list and now you're telling me to start eliminating wants." That's true, but only partially—the other wants are still there, they've just been postponed for the time being as lower priorities. And this does not have to be a one-time event—this is a tool for everyday use as your definition of success naturally evolves.

Run a "qualifier tournament" for each of your categories until you have the top priority for each. If you're having trouble deciding, choose anyway as if you had to, knowing that once you achieve the most important want, the next want will move into the spotlight.

Once you've completed these, you have a list of your *core wants*. These represent the most meaningful or highest priority wants in the various areas of your life. Now you're ready for the "main draw tournament" between these core wants using the same diagram displayed above. This may seem very difficult at first—these will inevitably be some hard-fought matches—but be patient and thoughtful, and go with your instincts. What you'll find is the essence of what success means to you, and with that knowledge of what purpose the business serves, the power of your personal intention rests solidly in your hands.

∿

Decide what you want, decide what you are willing to exchange for it. Establish your priorities.

—*H.L. Hunt*

Question:
Do I know what I am truly willing to exchange for the opportunity to be successful? What are my daily priorities to accomplish it?

Affirmation:
I prioritize my work each day to achieve my intended result.

∿

Breaking the Habit of Projection

As we saw in the case of Jim and Betty's presentation at the beginning of this chapter, if making a million dollars is *your* ultimate goal, it's easy to make the mistake of assuming that's what everyone else wants too. But if your goals are less extravagant, don't think you're off the hook—networkers with smaller-scale goals can err in the same way.

I learned a very valuable lesson about the importance of paying attention—without judging—in my early days of developing a network marketing business. You may remember this story from my book *Recipes for Successful Phoning—Scripts and Tips for Network Marketers.*

When I was building my organization, I often traveled to new areas to share the opportunity and help a new group build. I was traveling in one of the eastern states, when a consultant named Susan asked that I extend my trip to a neighboring city to personally meet one of her prospects. This prospect had actually been given to Susan as a lead from the company. Susan had done the proper follow up. She had phoned, sent information, and was at the point she felt a face-to-face meeting would help her prospect, Anne, make the decision to join our company. Susan lived quite a distance from Anne, and since I was going to be in her area, she thought it would be effective if I paid a visit.

So I took a commuter plane to Anne's town. She was gracious enough to pick me up at the airport and invited me to stay in her home for a few days while we discussed the possibility of her joining our company. As I stepped off the plane, I was anxious to meet her. I scanned the people at the airport trying to determine which one might be Anne when a lovely woman approached me and said, "Hi, I'm Anne. Are you Pat?"

I was with a cosmetic company, so image and appearance were very important. Typical of most distributors for our company, I made a quick evaluation as soon as I met Anne. "No makeup but good skin, understated hair style, simply dressed, and nice." Not *judging*, I told myself, just *observing*. We got into her car, a five-year-old economy car—not a judgment, just an observation—and I began chatting and getting to know her.

About ten miles later we pulled up in front of a massive stone building with a huge gate and iron fence surrounding it. I quietly *observed* that she must have an errand to do here. The building was so huge I thought it must be a public building of some sort, like a library. When we drove through the gate and parked, I asked why we were stopping there. Anne looked at me and calmly stated, "This is my home."

I stayed in a private wing with my own private living room, bath, bedroom, and kitchen. Anne's home had a dining room that could seat 50, without the leaf in the table, and there were two kitchens in the main house which I'm sure they needed to entertain 50 for dinner. Doesn't everyone?

Wow, was I ever off base with my "not judging, just observing" conclusions. The facts were that Anne's husband was a top executive of a major corporation and they were quite wealthy.

Anne told me how much she enjoyed our conversation about the products and the company. She admitted that, based on past conversations with Susan, she almost refused my offer to visit. Susan was young, enthused, and very motivated by the home award that our company offered as part of its compensation plan. Since Susan had two children and lived in a tiny two-bedroom apartment, this was a huge incentive for her, so of course, the home award became Susan's automatic opportunity button that she switched on for *everyone*.

Anne went on to explain the obvious. "As you can see, Pat, a $100,000 home award is of no interest to me. Actually, our summer cottage on the lake is worth much more than that. However, I do love these products and want to help others enjoy them, too."

I learned one of the most important lessons of my career that day. The lesson is that you *never* know where people are in life. Until you know what your prospects want *individually*, you can't recruit, train, or support them to achieve their goals—you can never build a win/win, mutually beneficial relationship. We are often so caught up with what network marketing has done or will do for us, we forget to be aware the many reasons why other people become involved.

The Dual Benefit of Defining Your Success

There are two wonderful benefits of learning to define success for yourself:

1) Your own tenure in the business will be longer, healthier, and more profitable.
2) Your effectiveness as a prospector and as a sponsor will dramatically increase.

After what you've read so far in this book, I'm sure number one comes as no surprise. But what about number two? The reason this is true is that your increased awareness of your *own* individual and nuanced reasons for being involved makes you more aware of what variance there will be among those you approach about the business and those you sponsor in. You'll know not to make the Jim and Betty mistake, and instead you'll develop adaptability in your approach so you'll be effective at connecting with any kind of person.

You won't suddenly find you have this skill overnight, of course, but you can speed its development by listening intently to stories about people whose lives have been enriched through their efforts in network marketing. Without these stories, you may not be able to imagine the possibilities that are open to you—and your prospects. Remember that network marketing is a relationship business and when you're with your prospects, the focus needs to be on them, not you.

The true stories that follow will help to feed your own evolving definition of success. You also will have much more versatility in relating to the many different motivations you'll encounter as your business grows. Consider these stories just a start. Be a student and seek out as many other stories as you can. As you read these network marketing biographies, let yourself expand the boundaries of how you've been thinking of network marketing so far—are there other ways it could serve your life or your loved ones that you haven't considered fully yet? With each story, ask yourself the following questions:

- What can this person's story teach me about defining and evolving what success means to me?
- What can I take away from this person's story to be better at identifying network marketing's potential value for people I meet?

Mark Eldridge's Story

Mark Eldridge's father had always been an entrepreneur. "He would make a fortune sometimes, and then a year later lose a fortune," Mark remembers. "He was always out there running one type of business or another. I saw him going in a cycle—on top of the world one year, the next year starting all over again." For most of Mark's childhood, his father was out of the home and away from the family working.

As an adult, Mark found that he shared his dad's entrepreneurial spirit. After three years in the 82nd Airborne, he left the military behind in favor of real estate investing and, a few years later, his own seminar business. "I was a promoter— I hired the speakers and I did all the work behind the scenes, from advertising to setting up hotels. I was making some great income."

However, Mark was working 90 to 100 hours a week, always trying to promote the next seminar. When his wife Karen became pregnant with their first child, it hit him that the business was consuming his life. Without a dramatic change, he'd miss out on his own kids' formative years, just like his father. "Being a workaholic is my natural upbringing, so it's very easy for me to fall into that rut."

His desire not to repeat the pattern led him to network marketing, but it was a family disaster that spurred him to pursue success in the industry with full, dedicated effort.

"A couple of weeks after our first son was born, we noticed that he was developing a growth on his upper lip. We had no clue what it was, so we went to the pediatrician, who didn't know what it was either. As it continued to grow, we finally went to a couple of experts and found out it was a tumor. It got to be the size of a marble, and we had his first surgery when he was only six months old. Unfortunately, the surgery did absolutely no good whatsoever and put him through a lot of pain and misery because it just kept growing.

"The next doctor we went to see literally told us that our son would never be normal, that we had to have half his face removed, and that he was going to be psychologically damaged for life. That's when I got mad. In this day and age with the technology we have, with the miracles that can happen, I knew there had to be a way for us to help our son. I realized at that point that I had to do something to find doctors who knew what they were doing and could take care of this challenge. I knew that not only would I need an ongoing income in order to do that, I'd also need time to go from city to city to find the best doctors.

"So I drew the line in the sand. I decided to do whatever I needed to do to make this happen, and I realized I had to use the vehicle of the network marketing industry to free up my time away from the seminar business to do what I had to for my son. That's when I really got serious. Up until then, I was failing miserably in the business. I didn't go to the meetings, I was reinventing the wheel trying to do it my way because I was successful in business. When I made that decision, I realized I had to get serious about finding out whatever I needed to find out in order to be successful in network marketing and truly have time freedom.

"That's when I started to see results and was able to start traveling around the country and reading medical journals to find information on my son's condition. It was only because of having that time to research that I was able to discover a doctor in Virginia who turned out to be one of the best in the world for that problem. By that point, my son had blisters in his mouth, he could hardly eat, and the tumor had grown to the size of a golf ball. It turned out this doctor could do the right thing for him and most of the challenges were eliminated literally overnight. After three operations over the next two and a half years, we were able to take care of everything, and today, he's one of the most happy, outgoing kids in his school."

After 18 months of focused building, Mark had developed a sizable organization and was able to spend less time on the business and more time with his family as he'd hoped when he first got started. With a second son and a young daughter now part of the family, this is more important than ever to the Eldridges. "We take two and a half months together in the summer and trips throughout the year to the mountains or to the beaches and still have income coming in. I'm proud to be going out there and helping a lot of other people accomplish the same thing.

"I feel one of the major reasons we're having so many challenges in society today is because parents aren't able to spend the time with their children that they used to when there was at least one parent at home. Now that both parents are having to work, there's even less time to spend with children. My wife and I schedule one day every single month that's devoted to whatever each child wants to do with that day, whether it's just going to the park or to Chuck E Cheese Pizza. We feel that's made a major difference in our family life. Most fathers—but even mothers these days—don't have the chance to spend two or three hours a day just playing with their newborn or toddler. We're happy to say that Sydney hasn't spent a single day in daycare. Knowing we can raise our own children instead of having someone else do the job is something this industry is rare in providing."

Mark acknowledges that there were challenging times, though, and that at the worst of them, the medical and financial pressures seemed to be driving the family apart. "It was seeing the bigger picture, having a plan, and being able to see the future as having the time and income freedom that pulled us through.

"What I've learned is that it boils down to understanding this isn't about the 'how to,' it's about the 'why.' There's so many people who come into the business and think they need to become masters at selling their product or making presentations, when frankly it's the opposite. It's having that vision of why are you building the business—what you want to accomplish once you're successful."

∽

Reflections

What initially attracted Mark to network marketing? Time. What did he see as the benefit of more time? Not missing out on his children's young years as his father had. But here's the interesting twist: What actually created an *intention* in Mark to succeed? His son's medical condition.

Do you have a goal that sounds good, that you'd like to have in your life, but it isn't getting you to pick up the phone? If you do, then you may be working with a goal that you *want* but don't *intend* to see become reality. Whether to take action or not is never a question when you intend to get a certain result. Is there something like this in your life that your business could help you accomplish? How about the people you know? Is there something of serious significance that network marketing could be a vehicle for making happen? Food for thought. . . .

～)

Joyce Oliveto's Story

As a naturopathic doctor who loves her work, Joyce Oliveto had no interest in starting a new business when she was first introduced to her company. "I've been extremely financially successful in my life and also emotionally fulfilled working in the natural healing field," she says. "I have been involved with network marketing since the early 1980s—with one company for 14 years—but never as the focal point of my life."

But today, she's one of her company's top leaders. In her own words, here's what changed and how her goals evolved:

"I was amazed at what I saw happen in my practice with people I'd worked with for years when I integrated the products. A responsibility developed for me because people wanted to start doing the business and my money grew very fast. That's when I decided I better learn how to do this right. I started to get serious about network marketing in March of 1996.

"I've always had a dream of serving children in the struggles they have in life—how they are used and abused and lied to—and as my network marketing income increased, I began to see more and more ways to do that. I'd already begun working with children in my practice, some as young as a year old with cancer, so I'd become very passionate about it. I decided to branch out from just working with children in the health field, to working with them on an emotional level in a camp setting. I figured I would rent a resort about two weeks out of every summer to do that.

"But what happened with me personally as my income grew was that my vision just continued to get larger and larger. I became much more passionate about it and became deeper in my purpose, realizing how many children I could touch.

"So about two years ago, I started to look for 80 acres of land with a lake on it in northern Michigan. That was just my starting point. It had to have a lake within the boundaries and it needed to be 80 acres. Why that number came into my head at the time I have no idea. We looked and looked, and nothing was coming up, and during that time, a client of mine who I had bought another parcel of land from, said, 'I know you've been looking for some land and something just came back on the market. It's about a mile and a half from your house, and it's 80 acres with a lake. I think it used to be a summer camp for kids and it might have some buildings on it.'

"I said, 'That's impossible, there's no such parcel with a lake near here.' But she assured me there was, so I decided to go see it. She gave me directions, and it literally was a mile and half from driveway to driveway. At first it appeared to be solid woods, but as I pulled in, I saw there was a house that the caretakers live in, a three-car garage, a pastor's quarters behind it—it used to be a church camp—and I made another turn and there was a cabin and a barn and another building. In the next area—and that's when I started crying—I looked up and saw a playground, a volleyball field, a baseball field, shuffleboard, and three big huge buildings. When I walked up to the buildings, one was a dormitory that had 44 bunk beds, counselors rooms, bathrooms, and the other building was a shower and bath building with an infirmary, five or six stalls, and showers on each end. The next building was the huge kitchen and activities room, and two more bedrooms, a bathroom, an office, and a storage room. It just kept going on—there are paths, a lake and a pond, apple orchards, pear trees, a bridge with an island in the lake. It's just all there.

"I called my friend right away and said I wanted it. It was the day before I was leaving for Dallas for a national company event, and two other people had put in a bid that same day. So she came over, and we quickly did all the paperwork for my bid, including my mission statement for my vision of the camp. I got on the plane and headed for the convention.

"Five members of the church that was selling it were going over the bids at 11 a.m. in Michigan at the same time we were in Dallas at a Sunday service that we have every Sunday after a national event. All weekend I'd asked everybody to pray for them to choose my bid. My realtor friend called me Sunday afternoon to say that they did choose it and were thrilled. I bought it a year ago, and it's a dream come true.

"I had a fulfilling and financially successful life before network marketing, but for me, this business has meant more fulfillment, more purpose, deeper purpose. I felt like I was on purpose already, but I now have more ability to actually give back to humanity. I believe you can change humanity if you work with the children. I now have a bigger reality, a grander scale for touching more children, really being able to contribute something to society, and actually being able to leave a legacy behind. I would love to see this duplicated around the world, and that's our goal.

"I mean, how much money do people need for themselves? I've had so many experiences in my life when I've had money and not been happy. We all know money doesn't always bring happiness, but I'll tell you—it sure brings joy and fulfillment to be able to help other people."

~

Reflections

Joyce was drawn to her network marketing company by how well the products worked for her patients. But as her story shows, that was only the beginning. She's a great example of how goals evolve. As she began to earn a greater and greater income in her network marketing business, things that would previously have seemed *too big* for her to achieve began to show up as realistic possibilities. As her means grew, so did her ability to imagine. She was able to create dramatic intentions, like her intention to form a camp, and believe it into existence.

Is there a contribution you've always wanted to make to others but felt you couldn't for time and money constraints? Is there something that would be truly meaningful in your life that network marketing can support? How about people you know? Do you have a friend who's an altruist at heart, couldn't care less about the money, but would be able to do much more with a business to fund the efforts?

~

Sandra Tillinghast's Story

From a position of security she can laugh about it now, but when Sandra Tillinghast first started in network marketing, she was a single parent with no child support. "I lived in Los Angeles—I got married when I was 22; had my son, John, when I was 25; and was divorced by the time he was three. I was young in a lot of ways," she recalls, "I was a survivor, I was strong, but I was young. In retrospect, though, I'm grateful for being a single parent at that age, because it really helped me get out of the victim mentality I sometimes see stopping people as much as anything else. They won't take accountability or responsibility. You have to lose that to be successful in network marketing."

A friend had told her about a network marketing cosmetic company, but Sandra blew the idea off. She started to reconsider, though, when, upon returning from a trip to Paris for her 30th birthday that she'd charged on her credit card. The reality of her financial situation began to set in. "I remember watching John as he slept at night and then going into my room and pulling out all the bills and the check book and thinking, 'We are circling the drain.' I thought back to when I was young, and I used to love to make up my aunts before they went out. My mom was one of 13 kids in her family, so some of my aunts weren't much older than I was. I loved making people look beautiful, and they were always so happy afterwards. When you look good, you feel better about yourself, so I decided to call my friend."

When she called, it turned out the friend had quit, but Sandra needed to earn $1,000 *fast,* so she met with someone at a management level to find out how. "In the early days, I didn't really believe in myself. I would go and be interviewed for jobs where somebody would say, 'you have the job or you don't have the job; you get paid this amount of money for this amount of work.' They would ask me about my credentials and my education level, but never about my dreams or my talents. In network marketing, people said to me, 'You can do it!'"

Within six months, she'd earned her first car.

"That taught me a lot," she says. "I started looking at my corporate job and how people treated me there and thought, 'For the amount of hours I'm doing my direct sales business and how much I'm making there versus how much I'm working and making in this job, I should quit my job and go full-time.' I resigned and told everyone what I was going to do, and they laughed at me. But about six months later, I went to see one of the secretaries who was a friend of mine, and I had a newer, fancier car from the company. She said, 'I don't understand—you have all this and you don't have a real job? You can do whatever you want whenever you want to do it?' I told her, 'Yes—I set my own hours, I work at my own pace, I'm my own boss, and I have a real business.' She couldn't get it."

But Sandra was thriving, and as she grew more successful, her aspirations grew. She set bigger goals for herself—even when pursuing them involved significant risk. "I was evolving, and I realized that company wasn't really it for me anymore. I'd started with that company because it was the only opportunity presented to me. Nowadays, people have so many choices, but back then I didn't. When I found the right company, the one I'm still with now after nine years, I quit—I gave my car back, no one came with me, and I started over from scratch."

At that point, success to Sandra was earning herself a Mercedes-Benz from her new company. After giving back her other car, she took a two-year lease on a white Ford Escort with an intention to earn the Mercedes by the time the lease was up. "One of my funniest memories is from this period when I knew I needed to build a new team and reach the Regional Vice President (RVP) level, before my lease ended, to earn the company car. I wasn't afraid to work, and I went all over the place in that Escort. I ended up reaching the level in just 20 months, and in my last month of qualification, I was driving to Laguna Beach one day, when I got pulled over by a policeman. At that point, if it didn't have to do with RVP or my son, I wasn't thinking about it. I'd become so focused, I'd let a few things slip—I had no registration because I was paying the bare minimum bills, my tags were expired, my license was expired, and here I was driving down the freeway.

"The policeman got out of the car and said, 'Lady, do you have any idea how much trouble you're in? I can take you to jail.'

"I started crying and giving him a sob story, and he asked, 'Do you have *anything* in your car that says who you are?' I picked up the company magazine from the seat beside me, which had my face on the cover. I said, 'This is me, and I'm going to become a Regional Vice President at the end of this month if you will just let me go. I have to be in Orange County to do a skin care class and I have to be there on time. If you just let me go, officer, I'm going to be somebody!'

"Believe it or not, he let me go!"

Even though her previous experience helped her to succeed faster this time, Sandra *was* afraid of not being able to do it again from scratch. Her self-confidence still wasn't very strong. It took a friend's challenge to get her through—a friend asked her once when she was feeling discouraged, "Have you given it your best shot?" Since she wasn't succeeding yet, there was no way Sandra would answer yes, so her friend suggested, "Why don't you give it your best shot and then quit?" Sandra agreed, with a plan *not* to quit until she was successful. Of course, when she reached that point, she didn't want to quit anymore.

"You know the phrase 'fake it 'til you make it?' It was almost like that—I believed in the company, I believed in the products, I believed in the people in my upline. And pretty soon I started believing in me. Now it's the other way around, and my whole life is different—I'm a better mother because of this business, I'm a better wife, a better friend, I can go and do anything. I don't have fear now."

With that personal transformation, her definition of success has changed yet again. "For me, real success is having a life filled with peace, ease, grace and prosperity. I feel like if I have prosperity, the money will be there. If I have peace, ease, and grace, my health will be there. And if I have balance, my family will be right. I'm like a little kid in this business. The same things thrill me after nine years with this company—signing people up, getting their business started, finding out they're coming to training, going to an elite party and seeing the smiles on people's faces when they're acknowledged, or having someone call to tell me about a great thing that happened to them."

As a leader in her company, Sandra still finds herself growing as a person and learning new things about the business—sometimes from the most unexpected people. One of the most important lessons she's learned recently began with an offhand remark to her husband.

"One night I was going down the list of people in my group and said to my husband, 'I'm so concerned about this one person. She's been in the company for a long time, and I can't believe she's still here with this minimal amount of success.'

"My husband looked at me and said, 'That's pretty arrogant of you to decide what her success is, don't you think? Based on what you told me about that person when she first came in, I'd guess that she's one of the most successful people in your group.'

"This struck me—and I started changing that belief immediately. I became unattached to the results. Before, I thought I knew what her success was supposed to be. If she wasn't getting that, I'd be frustrated—instead, I started letting it go. Nobody knows why another person really comes into the business except that person and God. When I stopped being like that, I got excited for everything to happen for her at her pace, and it was fun.

"Those of us in leadership roles can make the mistake of projecting things we don't know we're projecting and missing a lot of what's going on with the team. The bottom line is, people are really ready to move forward when they say, on their own, 'No more of this, I've had it.' Today, my goal is to help as many people as I can have *their* success."

～

Reflections

Sandra's reason for getting started in network marketing is extremely common: financial necessity. How many people do you know in situations similar to hers? Are you among them? She'd always been on shaky financial ground, but what finally caused her to develop an intention to make the business work? The realization that she was "circling the drain"—knowing she *had* to make it work. This may not be the most enjoyable circumstances for beginning a business, but the motivation can be extremely powerful as Sandra's story illustrates.

But even starting with nothing, Sandra's definition of success grew as she hit the smaller milestones along the way. For many people, the best place to start in network marketing *is* with a simple dollar-figure goal that will make an immediate difference in their lives. When I was building my network marketing business, I shared the opportunity with a lot of people who, more than anything, needed what I called "top-up money." They just needed more than their current job could give them, maybe an extra $1,000 a month, and weren't necessarily looking to replace their income. Surprising as it may sound, I found that many times those people who came in with smaller goals at first would actually see success faster, which would increase their belief, and they'd go on to make a six-figure income and give up the job they thought was their security. The people who came in wanting the big money from the start often didn't have the patience to stick with it and quit before they ever reached their lofty goal.

What difference could $1,000 more each month make in your financial life if you used it to pay off debt? If you invested it for your future? If you saved it for education or memorable travels? Spend some time giving this some thought and doing a little math. For now, though, let's turn to a love story from a couple who found each other in network marketing. . . .

∾

Steve & Melissa Huszczo's Story

Steve Huszczo was successful in a career he loved. As a professional chef living and working in Toronto, he trained apprentices, pleased hundreds of happy diners, and was even honored for his skill by being invited to serve as the head chef for the Olympics when Calgary hosted the games.

"I loved that industry," he says, "every plate that went out of the restaurant had my name on it, and there was a lot of pride involved."

His is an example, though, of how life can throw us a curve ball when we least expect it. In one of the most common and mundane parts of his job—lifting a box of chicken onto a freezer shelf—Steve ruptured two disks and ended up in the hospital for back surgery. The doctors told him he would recover, but he'd never be able to return to the physical demands of being a chef. In a day, his career was over.

"My life totally changed. When I first heard that I couldn't go back to my career, I was thinking, 'Why me?' Initially I rejected that prognosis and was sure that I'd eventually be able to go back to it, but it didn't take long for the realization to sink in. Every time I tried, I found I just physically couldn't do it, and it really took the wind out of my sails. One of my dreams my whole life was taken away from me, and I didn't handle it very well. I was in a lot of pain and kind of lost there for awhile. I ended up with a lot of other health challenges that my doctor told me would be with me the rest of my life."

Steve tried everything—from acupuncture to homeopathy to naturopathic medicine to European doctors—and eventually some friends introduced him to products from their network marketing company. Steve had typical negative misconceptions about network marketing, and at first he wouldn't return his friends' calls. But at that time, nothing meant more to Steve than restoring his health, so realizing he had nothing to lose, he reluctantly decided to give their recommendations a try.

Within six weeks he was feeling significantly better, and within two months, Steve no longer needed all the medication he'd been taking. He then became motivated to get the products for free. "I figured if I'm going to tell people about them, why not get paid for it?" He attended a presentation. . . .

"A lady stood up and give a testimonial that she just earned a $200 check, and in seeing how excited she was, I knew I could share this business with other people and get them just as excited. Initially, I started to look at the dollars, but it didn't take long for me to realize that the dollars weren't ultimately what I was going after—it was helping people. Because I had success with the products, I really wanted to share them with a lot of people."

Little did Steve know that the more involved he became in his network marketing business, the closer he was to discovering a most unexpected and wonderful benefit. He'd made a habit of always visualizing himself achieving whatever his next goal was at the time, and began to do the same for a potential romantic partner.

"I wrote out exactly what I wanted my future wife to be like," Steve explains. "In fact, I still have the five pages of detailed information I compiled about the woman I wanted to meet. I kept visualizing it, and one day as I walked onto a plane headed for my network marketing company convention, I saw Melissa—she just lit up like a light bulb and I instantly gravitated towards her. I knew the person she was sitting beside, and said, 'We gotta talk!'"

Melissa was also in the company, though at the time, still relatively new. As a financial administrator, she was drawn to the business plainly and simply for the numbers. "I understood the financial potential very quickly," she says. "I was at a point with my finance job and a whole lot of my life where I was thinking, 'Is this it? Is this life? There's got to be something better.' At the time, success would have meant not working until I was 65 years old and being able to enjoy life instead of going through the humdrum way that so many people do. I didn't want that to be me."

The two stayed up until four in the morning talking at the convention and began dating not long after returning to Toronto. After a year of romance and getting to know one another, Steve and Melissa were married on an island, followed by a month-long honeymoon. Today, four years after Steve first started in the business, he's healthy, married to the woman of his dreams, and living in what they describe as their "dream home on 24 acres of land with big windows that look out over water"—not exactly what he or Melissa originally bargained for when they independently decided to join network marketing.

"Sometimes people think you have to have the big homes and the million dollars," says Steve, "but when you look at it, the personal successes really mean so much more than the money, because when I lost my health, nothing else mattered. I gave up everything to get my health back to the point that I was in debt and had to borrow the money to start the business. Instead of going for the thousands or the millions of dollars from day one, it's focusing on the small, important successes that keep people on track.

"We have people in our organization who couldn't afford to put food on the table and now they're driving around in new vehicles and taking vacations. One person was a retired accountant forced to give up his practice of 36 years because of pain; in regaining his physical health with our products, network marketing offered him a new beginning. We've had mothers do the business to stay home with children, we have university students earn money for school, we had a man who lost his farm—someone who owed him money went bankrupt, and like a domino effect it made him go bankrupt too. He was forced to sell and go into driving trucks which kept him away from his family, so all he wanted from this business was to improve the quality of his family life."

"The simple fact that someone joins this business is a success," adds Melissa. "The fact that they speak to the very first person is a success. Success doesn't have to be defined by when and if you become a millionaire."

Of course, neither Steve or Melissa claims that achieving the security they now have was always easy. For Steve, the biggest challenge was rejection: "Because of my previous negative impressions of the industry, I didn't really see the power network marketing has to change lives. I realized that not everyone is going to join my business or my company or network marketing, and I became at ease with that. I also always surrounded myself with positive people, and that made a huge difference."

Melissa's biggest challenge was believing in herself and becoming confident enough to talk to people. It was with Steve's help that she decided to dedicate some time each day to developing herself and building her self-esteem. He gave her all the books and tapes that he'd used himself. "It's still not always easy for me," she admits, "but I work at it every day because I know that working on self-belief is a major part of doing this business."

Steve feels strongly about meeting people where they are. "A lot of companies want to put a high emphasis on finding that leader who's going to do it with or without you, but that's going for the three-percenters. Network marketing really is for everybody, but most importantly for the 97-percenters that start off simply looking for that extra few hundred dollars a week that will make a huge difference in their life. Often I see networkers giving too many statistics, using too many words people don't understand, and talking big dollar figures, but that just shuts them down. It doesn't seem real to them. I've learned to find out what their immediate needs are and base a business partnership on helping them achieve those first. I believe in showing people that they can achieve the $100 before they can achieve the $400, because if you don't do that, they're not going to see themselves making the thousands."

Looking back on how their own definitions of success have evolved, Steve and Melissa look forward now, saying, "We know we'll achieve what we need to, and we just want to be happy in the process. Success to us now is helping other people reach their goals, and nothing means more to us. When you get that phone call from somebody saying, 'Thank you, you've made a difference in my life,' it's the greatest feeling."

∽

Reflections

What brought Steve to network marketing? The intention to be healthy again. "Nothing else mattered," he said. And how about Melissa? She came for the income potential and a change. Her life felt too predictable, and she intended to do something about that—the timing was perfect. Looking back, though, they recognize that those early objectives are only a few of the many benefits they've gained through their involvement with this industry—each other topping the list!

How can this story inform the way you explain the potential benefits of network marketing? Have you faced any of the challenges they faced while getting their business off the ground? What does their definition of success have to offer how you think about your own?

∾

What Size Dreams?

The moment one definitely commits oneself, then providence moves too. All sorts of wonderful things occur to help one that would never otherwise have occurred. A whole stream of events issues from the decision, raising in one's favor all manner of unforeseen incidents and meetings and material assistance which no man could have dreamed would come his way. Whatever you can do or dream, you can begin it. Boldness has genius, power, and magic in it. Begin it now.

—Goethe

How do you define happiness? Where is the fine line between being true to who you are and genuinely content, and making excuses not to bring more out of yourself than what's really there? Do you have more possibilities? Are you sitting there happy as a clam on the outside, but inside really wanting more but not believing you can *achieve* more on the path that life seems to be taking you?

The networkers whose stories you just read spend a good

amount of time contemplating these questions. There's no right answer for everyone, and only you can answer for yourself. Consider them, let them roam around in your head while you read this book. Make things simple by first zeroing in on goals that feel tangible—what you want to gain *first* from your efforts. It's your responsibility to decide what your goals are, and you have no obligation to anyone to dream bigger or smaller than you choose. Of course, almost everyone starts off wanting to be a top distributor. Your upline, having traveled the road to financial success, sees great potential in you—probably even more than you see in yourself. The key here is that if someone handed any of us a six-figure income for free, we'd happily accept it, but *news break*: A six-figure income is anything but free—it requires serious commitment and work—and the thought, "Wouldn't it be great!" doesn't tap into the genuine, accessible desire that inspires action. This is why I suggest thinking about what you'd like to achieve now, that you can "see from where you're standing."

~⌒

No *wind favors him who has no destined port.*
—Michel De Montaigne

Question:
Do I have clear and concise goals for my life and business? Am I following them?

Affirmation:
By setting clear and concise goals, the ship of my business stays on course.

~⌒

Many networking leaders have complained to me that the hardest challenge in this business is getting people to see the possibilities. I certainly understand and remember being frustrated with that myself. I would see my new distributors' potential and want so much for them. I would work and work to try to push them forward in their success journey, and yet there was always someone who wouldn't so much as budge forward on that path. It would become difficult for me to understand sometimes, because I wanted all of them to see what they could have if they applied themselves to this business.

I recall one particular time feeling extremely frustrated with a distributor, because no matter what I did, I could not get her to achieve the targets and goals we set for her. (The key word: "goals *we* set for her.") I had done everything I knew how to and *still* couldn't get her to move forward. I was even starting to question my leadership. Yes, doubt crept in for me, and I was doubting my own ability to lead more than her ability to achieve. I was allowing her lack of achievement to affect my belief system. I confided this frustration to a mentor of mine at the time, explaining how it seemed this distributor just could not or would not see what she could have if she only applied herself. I asked, "Why can't she see this?" and he very wisely answered me, "Well dear, that's where she is in life." I learned to respect that statement for a few reasons.

First, if your sponsor can see you as a top person in the company and it doesn't feel like you, how can you be enrolled in an effort to become that person? It's frustrating and unpleasant to try to be someone else. If you don't define your own goals, if you don't make the choice yourself, you won't own your business. However, if it doesn't feel like you and you would *like* for it to, then identify what success feels like to you *now*. When I first started in network marketing, I wanted spending money, I wanted not to run out of money before I ran out of week, I wanted a car, and I wanted life to be better for my children. If a fortune-teller had told me I would make the income I eventually made, it would have scared me, because I not only wasn't there in life, I didn't yet have enough belief in my abilities to set that high of a goal. Getting to that place was an evolution. My *now* was to be home when the kids got off the school bus and have a car to drive when Ollie was at work. But as my children grew, so did my business—my life and my needs changed. I grew, the family grew, my business grew, and it all happened simultaneously. Eventually, I began traveling and was away from the family in short business trips, but traveling when the children were younger wouldn't have fit—it would not have felt like success to me then.

Second, I learned what I've been emphasizing to you here— that goals grow. We are naturally upwardly mobile, and when you achieve your current definition of success, you'll find that your goals expanded with your skills and competence. You don't have to be locked into whatever your goal is today. It can and should evolve as your accomplishments increase. Sometimes achieving a series of smaller goals is the best way to increase the belief in yourself that will lead you naturally to bigger goals down the road. As Westerns author Louis L'Amour put it, "There will come a time when you believe everything is finished. That will be the beginning."

～♪

The best thing about the future is that it comes only one day at a time.
—Abraham Lincoln

Question:
Am I staying focused on what I can do today, or am I living for "someday"?

Affirmation:
By doing what needs to be done today, I create a happy and abundant future for myself and my family.

～♪

SECTION TWO

The Gift

The Gift

A fter learning to define your own success, one of the most important things you can learn in this business is how to effectively communicate to *others* that network marketing can serve whatever goals *they* want. This chapter outlines my favorite technique for doing just that as well as the mindset you need to approach such communication to the best mutual advantage for you and your prospects.

Network Marketing: The Gift

I like to equate sharing the network marketing opportunity with giving someone a custom-made gift. It is a gift that can be whatever they like. John Kalench reminded us, in his classic book *Being The Best You Can Be In MLM*, that the dictionary defines "presentation" as a performance (noun) or to offer another a gift (verb). He goes on to explain that you may not always walk away with your prospects' agreement to try your product or sponsor into your business, but if you're clear that your presentation is a gift, you can always feel good about offering it—whether they accept it or not.

I've found that those who have this gift mentality become tremendously successful. Their confidence and ease in sharing the business is magnetic—people respond to sincerity and detachment far better than nervousness and desperation. Sometimes the people with this attitude don't even understand why others find the business to be so difficult. For them, talking about the business and inspiring others to explore the opportunity becomes natural and fun.

Whatever approach your sponsor took in sharing network marketing with you, I hope you realize now what an incredible gift that person gave you. What's so wonderful about this gift is that it can be anything you want it to be. Think of it as a gift box that contains for each of us what *we* would like to receive. Take a moment and visualize this gift. . . .

Close your eyes and let your imagination run wild. Pretend that you have a magic bottle and in this bottle is a genie. This genie can pop out and fill your network marketing gift box with anything you can dream up. Picture a *huge* present . . . a gift box elegantly wrapped in the most gorgeous paper you have ever seen and topped with a massive and exquisite bow (remember, presentation is everything!). Start visualizing all the things the opportunity you've chosen can provide. What gifts will you fill your gift box with?

As your imagination fills it with wonderful dreams, you are adding a visual component to your definition of success. One of my favorite exercises in my workshop involves actually making such a gift box and filling it with representations of what the network marketing gift means to you. Once you've done this, it is equally powerful to share your gift box as part of presentation to help others visualize what accepting the gift you offer could be like for them. Here's how. . . .

Receiving the Gift and Giving to Others

This powerful yet fun and casual presentation technique can serve you in defining success for yourself and in assisting others to do the same. Begin by finding items that are either replicas of or symbolic of things you have either already achieved through network marketing or that you intend to achieve in the future. What goes in the gift box is up to you. If you decide to make one, just remember, it has to be gorgeous. If you make it a portable size, you can then use your gift box in two valuable ways:

1) At group or individual presentations you can convey to prospects how many different and individual ways network marketing success can benefit them.
2) At a training or a meeting with your group to lend a visual effect to what you teach them about defining their own success and the importance of approaching prospects with the attitude that network marketing is truly a gift.

To give your creativity a boost, here's what I put in my gift box to represent what network marketing gave to me—it helped me to tell my story and illustrate what success was to me and how it evolved as I built my organization. I'd open the lid of my gift box to find . . .

- **A miniature airplane.** This represented to me the gift of travel. Until I got involved with network marketing, I'd never been on an airplane. I was 24 years old when I started, and the most I had traveled was by bus or train. I also put in mementos from my travels around the world—a plastic lei representing one of my many trips to Hawaii; an Eiffel tower replica to remind me of those two weeks in Europe; brochures from five-star hotels worldwide. In the beginning, just to fly on a plane felt like success. Now to fly first class is what success feels like to me. I get upset when I fly coach now. If I have to go coach class, I walk past those in first class and boldly state, "I usually sit here." I no longer feel successful except in first class. My, how life changed!

- **Three little pieces of paper rolled up with ribbons.** These represented diplomas—the education I was able to fund for my family through network marketing. At one time, I had two children and a husband in college. Because of network marketing, I was able to allow my husband to take a leave from his job and complete his education as well as help the children get their degrees.

- **Faux jewelry.** This represented to me all of the fine jewelry I've earned. I *love* jewelry—I believe it was put on this earth for me and others to enjoy its beauty. I just love being surrounded by beautiful things. These pieces of jewelry I earned were recognition items—trophies of a sort for goals set and achieved. I personally always have liked the kind of trophies I could wear. I love looking at my fingers adorned with these sparkling reminders as I say to myself,

"I'm good!" My "trophy" collection is extensive thanks to network marketing.

- **A dish rag.** You may not think this is glamorous, but I put a dish rag in my gift box to remind me that in network marketing, I was able to earn enough money so I didn't need to do housework. One of the early definitions of success to me was being able to have household help. I must have clean and tidy surroundings and I love a clean house. In order for me to do all that I wanted—run my business, have family time, *and* a clean house—something had to be sacrificed. Housework took time, and I quickly realized that time could be purchased. This was one of my first "ah ha's" after starting my business. If I hired someone else to clean the house, I accomplished three things. First, I had the clean house that gave me a sense of peace. Second, I could spend Saturday with the children rather than doing housework. And third and also important, I was contributing to the workforce of America. There are people who love cleaning, and since I'm not one of them, I can allow others to do what they like doing and I can do what I like doing—spending Saturday with my family.

I learned this family balance lesson very early on. I made sure that every Monday I had a retail sales appointment to show my product because I had the intention of selling enough every Monday to pay for a housekeeper. It was easy for me to have one good sale to afford that. It certainly made sense to me—I spent one to two hours selling, took that money, and had eight hours with my family on Saturday. Just another way network marketing lets you leverage your time. (On a side note, if you're married and your spouse usually does the housework, give him or her this gift from network marketing—you could score big points here with the entire family with all those free Saturdays together.)

- **Miniature automobiles.** These of course represented to me that initial reason I got involved in network marketing— to get my own car. They also represented the other cars I was able to earn through my business over the years, and help *others* earn too, with great satisfaction.

- **Bank books, pictures of friends, and on and on. . . .**

Can you now visualize my gift box? When I shared it with others, I would say, "May I show you a gift that someone once gave me?" Then I would carefully open the lid, laying it to the side so as not to disturb the beautiful bow. I would bring out each item one by one. I'd show them everything in my gift box, explaining what each item was and what part of success it represented to me.

When I finished, I'd put everything back in the box, carefully and gently, again putting the gorgeous bow back on, and say, "I would love to give you this gift, this wonderful gift of network marketing. It will then be *your* gift. I will be your business partner and guide you in filling it with whatever you wish. However, you have a choice. A mentor once taught me, 'Life is about choices'— if you choose not to take the gift, not to take the lid off and find out what it offers for you inside, that's your choice. We'll still be friends, but I sincerely wish for you all that this gift and opportunity have to offer. Tell me, what would you fill your gift box with?"

This closing question will begin your process of identifying their "wanna" right from the beginning.

It's in Your Attitude

Whether you decide to use this technique in your presentations or simply to fuel your own vision, the attitude it displays is one you should strive always to maintain. That network marketing is a gift is the truth, *and* the results you'll find when you communicate this will prove its value.

Once you start thinking in these terms, approaching the act of prospecting as offering a gift that people can take or leave, you won't feel rejected anymore if they say "no." If they are not at the right time and place in life to take the lid off and accept it, that's okay. Just stay in touch as life changes, and feel free to offer your gift at another time. So now that *you* understand what letting others know about network marketing can provide for them, don't keep the gift to yourself.

I am so thankful that Frances shared this gift with me so many years ago, despite my reluctance to take the lid off and explore. My life and the lives of everyone in my family were changed for the better. Unfortunately, I don't think Frances really understood what a gift it was, because three months later, she quit. She quit network marketing—just didn't have enough belief to get past 90 days. What a shame. She lost years and years of bonuses and overrides from my success. I regret she didn't make it to payday and benefit as fully as she could have; nonetheless, I still send her a thank you card every now and then. Every time I got a new car, took a trip, or got an especially nice bonus check, I would thank her, because it was a wonderful thing that she did for me—sharing the gift of network marketing.

Personal Growth

One gift that most of us unexpectedly receive from our experience in network marketing is personal growth, though it's harder to convey this to people than it is to explain how the business lets you travel or spend more time with family. It's an immaterial and yet no less substantial benefit of our industry—you can't help but grow and develop as a person as you grow and develop your business.

We've discussed at length how goals change over time, and I want to emphasize here that it doesn't happen in a vacuum—it's growing as a person, in part, that causes your goals to evolve. The two happen simultaneously. If you're not very far along yet, you may have to take my word for this one, but I'm sure your upline will back up this assertion based on their experience. Network marketing is like embarking on one of the best self-improvement courses available. As you start to associate with positive people, read positive books, attend positive seminars, and spend time in this environment of people stretching limits and achieving goals, intending to better their lives and then doing so, you can't *help* but start developing as a person.

The personal advancement you experience will also extend to your family, your friends, and everyone around you. What a great side benefit. Major corporations always list all aspects of what they offer their employees in benefit packages, so list personal development in your network marketing benefit package.

I think you'll also find that personal growth has a balloon effect on your belief in yourself and your abilities—the subject of a chapter to come—and it's this increased belief that will propel you toward your current goals and beyond.

To begin your personal and business development, identify what you want now, and re-evaluate it along the way. Everybody brings different things to the table, so wherever you are in life, start there—and trust the process. Love yourself as you are now, but fall passionately in love with the person you intend to become.

ᴖ

Take care to get what you like, or you will end up liking what you get.

—George Bernard Shaw

Question:
Do I know what I want from life?

Affirmation:
I allow myself to know what I really want from life and I go get it.

ᴖ

SECTION THREE

Belief in Network Marketing

SECTION THREE

Belief in Network Marketing

I f you read the previous chapter thoughtfully, by now you have a clear idea of what personal success in this business would look like for you. But if you're like so many others who get started in network marketing, you dread the idea of actually *talking* to people about it—which is something you must do if you want to make the meaningful changes you've defined.

I'll be blunt with you by letting you know that the obstacle that holds more people back than any other in network marketing is lack of belief and conviction in their decision to get involved in the first place. I focus a whole section on this because you can know every detail about what to do and how, but if your belief in the industry is weak, you'll feel uncomfortable doing the necessary activities to succeed—so you won't. Perhaps you haven't even been honest with yourself, let alone your upline, about just how much this discomfort is holding you back. People will ask you what you do, and you'll mumble under your breath, whether you've read every how-to book in the industry or not. Until you can walk out on the sidewalk and scream happily to the world at the top of your lungs that you are proud of your decision, you won't be able to share the excitement that will draw others to join you. If you're secretly ashamed of your business—your actions and self-presentation will reflect it. Once you become proud of the network marketing industry, though, what used to feel like the scariest thing in the world to talk to people about will be the easiest and most natural. And don't worry—this is a natural part of the process.

The biggest thing you have to be clear about is that everything in this business starts with you. That's not to say you don't need or won't get support, but your success starts with *you* understanding and embracing your choice. Only you can do that, and fortunately, it's not hard—there are more than enough reasons to be in love with network marketing.

Taking Pride in Network Marketing

At the time of this writing, being a part of network marketing means being a part of a worldwide, 25-million-person, $84-billion industry. That's substantial. There's a non-profit lobbying association in Washington, the Direct Selling Association, devoted exclusively to supporting the growth and promoting public understanding of this industry as well as protecting the rights of networkers against legislators who may still have incorrect and outdated negative assumptions about it. Founded in 1910, DSA represents more than 140 companies that manufacture and distribute goods and services sold directly to consumers. The Association's stated mission is "To protect, serve and promote the effectiveness of member companies and the independent business people they represent. To ensure that the marketing by member companies of products and/or the direct sales opportunity is conducted with the highest level of business ethics and service to consumers." I recommend bookmarking the DSA website, *www.dsa.org*, for the access it gives you to positive and legitimate third-party information, as well as the latest sales figures available at any given time.

At a workshop I gave recently, we spent a long time talking about the size and scope of the impact network marketing is having on the business world and the lives of individuals. Afterwards, a young woman came up to me and said, "You know, I never thought about the industry that way before. I'm with a little company doing just a few million dollars a year. I haven't been very successful yet, but when I think of myself as being part of something bigger, then I take more pride." She told me that her grandmother had been constantly telling her to "get a real job," and after attending my Prospecting Gems workshop, she went back to her grandmother and told her that she was part of an $84-billion industry. "Ever since then," she said, "my grandmother has had a whole new respect and asks me how my business is going and even sends me leads. Thank you for helping me understand the bigger picture of network marketing. I feel such pride to be part of such a tremendous global industry."

And well she should. Twenty-five million people worldwide producing $84 billion is extremely impressive. These figures from the DSA, which is the best measuring stick we have, definitely represent the industry activity. If $84 billion in goods and services are being moved worldwide through network marketing, do you think that impacts the world economy? Absolutely! If it went away, do you think Wall Street would notice? It would make an impact on the economy of the world. If you became a part of an $84-billion company, would you be embarrassed about it? Would you whisper the name of it or apologize for it? No, because I doubt you'd see a reason to do so. Is it really so different in network marketing?

Network marketing is indeed an exciting industry, and this is an especially exciting time to be involved. Yet, I know you can hear that all day long (and probably have) while still not feeling 100 percent certain about it. What I'm going to ask you to do is put all of your own personal objections out on the table so that you can check them out in the light, deal with them in whatever way is necessary, educate yourself, and move on to achieving what you started for. Many of you may think, "Well, *I* can see that it's a great industry, but . . ." when people you respect put it down, your confidence in your own assessment goes down. Let's consider network marketing's bad reputation.

Why the Bad Reputation?

As you no doubt found out with your first couple of contacts—or if you haven't made any yet, be prepared—there are people out there who think network marketing is "a scam." That opinion is changing as the industry grows, but unfortunately this misconception is still present. There are four primary reasons for this:

#1 Unrealistic Expectations

A lot of people have been told that network marketing is a "get-rich-quick" business when the truth is that, for the vast majority of people, it's not. Unscrupulous networkers, however, have done the disservice to the industry of selling the big dream by giving the impression, implicitly or explicitly, that you can succeed without effort. This is simply a falsehood, but one that some people are eager to believe since it sounds so good. As a result, there are unfortunately many people who come into the business with expectations so unrealistic that disillusionment is only a matter of time.

The fact is that network marketing is like any other business—you have got to pay your dues, plan your work, and work your plan—there is no free lunch. You need to invest time, but those who've developed unrealistic expectations usually draw the conclusion that if they've been in a month and they're not rich yet, network marketing must "not work." You also need to invest money; even though it's a fraction of what you'd have to invest in any other business offering comparable earning potential. People with unrealistic expectations often resist spending a dime on their personal or business development, drawing the same conclusion they did about time: "if money's not coming in already, network marketing must not be legitimate."

So without the correct perspective on what it takes to succeed, these people frequently quit, feeling cheated and depressed, never fully understanding, let alone experiencing, the power of the business they almost pursued.

#2: Survival of the Fittest

Will everyone make it? No—not everyone has the dedication and the drive it takes. This is the case in any field of endeavor. The people who've been successful worked hard—they didn't just wake up one day and think, "I will be part of the top 20 percent in my field" and suddenly have it be true. They paid their dues when most people, no matter what their business, aren't willing to.

What's so wonderful about network marketing is that anyone *can* succeed—the opportunity is equal for all of us, no matter our background, gender, age, ethnicity, experience, or education. That does not mean, however, that everyone *will* succeed. Being an entrepreneur is challenging, and for many people, what they have to do to succeed doesn't prove worth it to them. They're more comfortable remaining where they are in life.

Does this mean it's a flaw in network marketing that not everyone succeeds? Of course not—the industry offers the same opportunity for all, but success is an individual decision.

#3: Ill Effects of Illegal Companies Posing as Legitimate

Over the past 50 years, there have been numerous cases of companies that were *not* legitimate, ethical network marketing companies, but posed as if they were. People without enough knowledge to distinguish good from bad have been taken advantage of by such companies—their dreams dashed, their money lost, their efforts wasted. Unfortunately, a few unethical companies can do substantial damage to the industry's reputation; people make the inaccurate assumption that *all* companies with a multi-level pay structure must be scams if they encountered one that truly was.

To put this in perspective, if someone told you they'd been to a terrible doctor and all doctors should be avoided because they're all alike, would you consider the blanket statement a credible one?

There are bad apples in every business. The DSA is the absolute best and most articulate source for describing what constitutes a legitimate company and what does not. The organization is devoted to clarifying the distinctions between schemes and the many wonderful, ethical, and impressive network marketing and direct sales companies providing valuable products, services, and opportunities to people.

#4: Bad Press

Someone quits his company angrily because his expectations proved unrealistic—he feels misled and mistreated and calls the local newspaper to complain.

Somebody else gives the business a "try," but finds it to be too difficult, feels frustrated and disappointed, blames network marketing rather than themselves, and complains to the local TV station.

The media loves scandal, and these examples simply illustrate how easy it is for negative stories—true and false—to show up in newspapers, magazines, and TV programs. And people tend always to remember and *repeat* bad news far more often than good news. It doesn't matter that those who gave it a try and quit have only themselves to blame. But when people get involved in a network marketing company with big dreams that don't come to fruition for *whatever* reason, it's a painful experience. The network marketing opportunity is unique in the way it re-instills hope in people's lives. When people speak negatively about the business, that's usually what they're really talking about—the experience of losing hope when they gave up and quit. The truth, though, is that the industry is booming and growing and becoming a stronger part of the world economy all the time—with or without the naysayers.

Fortunately, there is more positive press for network marketing now than ever before, and more and more people have come to understand what the business is about.

The Opportunity and You

Having peeked behind the curtain of our industry's bad reputation, I think you'll agree that much of the information is unreliable and disconnected from the truth about the industry. Charles King certainly does. This University of Chicago professor, who developed the first network marketing certificate program, declares in his excellent book *The New Professionals* that "Network marketing . . . has entered the new millennium with a fresh image as a place for winners." Indeed, as he points out, "There has been a distinct movement of traditional corporate America buying network marketing divisions, establishing start-up network marketing organizations, or developing strategic alliances/joint ventures with network marketing companies as a planned strategy of diversification into this lucrative distribution arena." With an understanding of how and why people have formed false and outdated impressions, you can feel confident to answer their objections.

Now let's consider some of the reasons why I and so many other people have come to love this industry—I invite you to join us. Twenty-five million people worldwide lend credibility to your choice to get involved, but more than that, you have to genuinely feel that this is an opportunity you *want* if you're going to convey confidence to others.

Network marketing is a means of distribution straight from the company and the manufacturer—which sometimes are one and the same—to the distributor, to the consumer. All of the middlemen are taken out. Most products that are sold in network marketing are products that need special explanation or education for the consumer—which is where *your* opportunity exists. As DSA President Neil Offen puts it, "I see recognition that the direct selling industry provides a wonderful supplemental income source or a career opportunity to be one's own boss and directly relate effort to reward, assisted in these endeavors in a symbiotic and synergistic relationship with solid, ethical, and technologically advanced support organizations, i.e. the direct sales companies of the future."

As more and more people are understanding the concept of personal leverage—creating maximum rewards for our time and money—the caliber of people being drawn to network marketing is rising all the time. We have surgeons, engineers, business executives, you name it, we have it in this business today. And they are all here for the same reason. They simply want inner peace, and they can't get it from just making money. The problem is that every time their "psychic" income goes up, their monetary income goes down. In other words, if they take the time away from work in order to add more value to their personal life, they lose monetary value in equal proportion. The same happens in reverse—if they work and work to earn more money, it's usually at the cost of their personal life and well-being. What's happening now is that people like you are starting to see that in network marketing, we've found a way to strike a balance.

Why You Have to Love Network Marketing—Not Just Your Company

It's common in this industry for people to justify keeping their personal objections about network marketing by feeling affiliated to their company *only*—not to network marketing, the means of distribution. I assert, however, that when you're out there talking to people, you must be sold on the industry of network marketing just as much as you are on your company. Why? Because the people you speak with don't know your company from any other. If you don't believe in the value of network marketing itself, you can't meet the naysayers. They may know you or they may not, but if they are not open to network marketing's means of distribution, it doesn't matter what company you chose to affiliate with. You have to be able to convey enthusiasm and conviction about the industry, not just *your* business.

That's what networkers often don't understand. In my view, direct sales and network marketing are the *opportunity* and the company you choose to represent is the *vehicle* you will "drive" to take advantage of that opportunity. Just as there are a lot of different vehicles out there on the road, there are a lot of network marketing companies from which to choose. You can find everything from the Hyundais to the Rolls-Royces, both in automobiles and in companies.

When shopping for an automobile, some people prefer cars with windows that roll down manually; some prefer the power buttons. The same is true of looking for features in the company that you choose. You will decide and choose what you are looking for in a company and in a product. Let me illustrate this concept— that network marketing is your opportunity and the company you choose is your vehicle—with a personal story and an analogy.

After three months of extensive research and shopping for a new automobile, I finally made my purchase. I had test-driven everything available that had the features I was looking for. For instance, I wanted leather seats, a 12-CD changer in the trunk, power *everything*, and various other bells and whistles I felt I "needed." I got all my features, loved my new car, and was quite happy with my decision.

When, as with any car, it came time for me to take it in for maintenance, the dealership was kind enough to give me a loaner car while mine was in for service. I was pleased to be provided with alternative transportation and drove off in the loaner car for the day.

Well, it didn't take me long to discover that this loaner car was not my car of choice. I arrived home complaining: "I can't believe this car. It has handles for rolling the windows down. I didn't know they still even made handles. It has cloth seats, and there are not any power features at all. I went to move the seat with the manual seat adjustment and almost catapulted myself through the windshield! And to top it off, there's not even a CD player."

After several minutes of my ranting and raving about this car, my husband reminded me, "Gee, Pat, there was a day when you would have loved to have that little car," and I thought to myself, "Well, not any more." He went on to point out that it *did* get me where I needed to go that day. I quickly snapped back, however, that "I didn't feel special in this car and it isn't the model that suits me anymore." I just couldn't wait to return the loaner car to the dealership. In truth, it *was* very dependable—it did provide transportation for me that day and there was nothing wrong with it—it just wasn't for me.

Just as no new car is "right" or "wrong," no company is right or wrong—just different. You have to find the one with the features that are comfortable for you. You may run into people while you're prospecting who say, "Oh, I've done that network marketing and it doesn't work." When I hear this, I think of the vehicle analogy. I doubt that if their car broke down and wouldn't run anymore that they would say, "Well that's that. Cars aren't any good, don't work. Here I am stuck home for the rest of my life." Of course not! They would immediately see if the vehicle could be repaired or go shopping for a new one.

If they didn't simply quit network marketing too soon, they may have chosen a vehicle that broke down on them, a "car" that didn't serve them or which included features that weren't right for them. They didn't understand that it wasn't network marketing that served them wrong—the means of distribution is still good and provides unlimited opportunities.

Now that you understand this, what you'll do is invite them over to test-drive your opportunity. How do you do that? Test-driving your company means sampling the products, attending meetings, having a three-way call, etc. It could be your company isn't the right one for them either, but it doesn't mean it's wrong, just not right for them. That's the way network marketing companies are. Some just aren't the best fit for certain people. Every suit doesn't fit the same person, different sizes, different shapes, doesn't mean the person's wrong and the suit's right, they just don't fit. The same is true of network marketing. The means of distribution, the opportunity is not wrong. It just means that everyone has to find the vehicle that's right for them.

With anything I am passionate about, whether it's a line of shoes or my favorite restaurant, the first thing I want to do is tell people about it. It's the same with network marketing. If you understand the concept, that's when you get the idea that you have something you want to give everybody—the first step in having people accept it.

It's Easier Now Than Ever

Many people have gone before to pave the path for you and the next generation of networkers—they started when the path was rough and undefined, made things better along the way, and gave the industry credibility by succeeding despite the many challenges they faced. They proved that it could be done and made it easier for the people who follow in their footsteps.

As a result, you've come to this business at a time when it is easier to be successful than ever before. Some of the obstacles the early pioneers of network marketing had to face have been entirely eliminated, primarily through technological innovation. Fortunately, technological advantage is readily available as well as cost-effective for everyone. Building your business was slow in the early days compared to the speed with which people are able to network and communicate today.

For example, you can have three-way calling on your telephone for a minimum investment, and it's available to everybody. I can three-way you in, you can three-way someone else, and so on in a chain until you can get about six people on the same telephone call. For larger groups, conference calling has revolutionized the way teams can work together over long distances. That service is also relatively inexpensive. I am regularly on calls with 100-plus people on the line from all over the world, which is a huge change from when I got started in network marketing. It used to be extremely difficult to recruit beyond your own backyard. Getting information to people by standard mail was our only option, which meant your prospects waited a week for what can now be sent instantly over the Internet. Some companies are even making all of these things available as a support package so that it can be done in the most cost-effective way possible under one umbrella.

There is also more validating information available now than ever in the industry's history. Most of it didn't even exist ten years ago, let alone 20 or 30 years ago when I got involved. Become a student of the industry. Arm yourself with information. If you only get excited about your company's product and compensation plan, but don't have solid information about network marketing, you are setting yourself up for challenges that just aren't necessary. It's your belief in network marketing that will feed your self-belief in the early stages of building your business.

Versatility

How many people do you know who run out of money before they run out of week? We all know how common this problem is and how much stress it can cause. That's exactly why I joined. My husband and I were living payday to payday at the time. We were a young couple with young children and a mortgage, and it wasn't easy. In today's economy, most couples don't have much choice about whether or not both will have to work. Even with two incomes, it's not always enough for the quality of life they want.

One doesn't have to want to be a network marketing superstar to reap genuine benefits from being involved. For so many people, just a few hundred extra dollars each month could make a radical difference in their lifestyle and security. How many people do you know who don't have even $100 a month to put toward their retirement? There are people in their forties, fifties, and sixties only just realizing they're going to get old. Today, younger people are beginning to think about it, too. Without network marketing, many people would have no way to create an income stream to fill the gaps. Will everyone take advantage of it? Sadly, no, but it's absolutely worth it for the smart people who do.

SECTION FOUR

Belief in Yourself

Belief in Yourself

Most people's lack of confidence comes from doubts about the industry, but even if your belief in network marketing is solid, you're still likely to find yourself in situations that can shake your confidence and deplete the strength of your intention from time to time. I call them "Maytag moments." Wait a minute—what do washing machines have to do with network marketing? You may be too young to remember the old Maytag washer repair commercials. They pictured a friendly, kind soul of a man sitting patiently by the telephone. He would sit there at his great big desk, day after day, waiting for the phone to ring so he could go out and repair someone's broken Maytag washing machine. Days and days would pass as he faithfully waited for the calls that never came. You see, Maytag was advertising in this humorous way that their machines were *so* dependable, you never needed to call the repairman. Very clever. Maytag did a great job of gathering sympathy for this repairman as "the loneliest repairman on earth."

That was probably ten or 15 years ago, but his loneliness stuck in my mind so much that now when I think of how lonely is lonely, my mind goes back to that commercial. Funny how certain memories stay with you and signify such totally different things for different people. I am sure that Maytag would be pleased that many years later, I have not forgotten their commercial. The ad executives certainly should be getting residuals from it—although I doubt they are. Hopefully they have found network marketing by now and are getting their residuals in a different way. (Sorry, just couldn't resist the opportunity to throw in that commercial of my own. I told you I was overjoyed about this industry.)

The point of this washing machine lesson is to know that no matter what great organization you are a part of, no matter what wonderful upline, sideline, or downline you have, you are bound to experience a few lonely "Maytag Moments" now and again in your business. All of a sudden, some doubt will creep in, and you will feel all alone in your decision to be in network marketing. You may feel you've encountered an obstacle you just can't get over, around, or through. You may doubt your decision, your product, your company, your opportunity, and most certainly yourself.

While the moments always pass, they're dangerous for networkers in the early stages of the business. These are the times when people think most seriously about giving up on their dreams and quitting. To prevent this from happening to you, you have to find ways to overcome that doubt and push through to the other side where success is waiting for you. Remember, a winner and a loser both have doubts and both get knocked down—it's just that the winner has learned how to get up faster.

So leave those lonely moments to Maytag—they can afford them; you can't. You are probably thinking, "Easier said than done.

What I need to know is *how* to increase my belief." The rest of this chapter is devoted to the answer: my six strategies for doing just that.

Six Strategies for Building and Maintaining Belief

When we talk about belief, sometimes the language can get pretty vague. It's hard to express in words exactly how belief grows and how it can rise on a good day and fall on a bad day. One thing's for certain—many people don't feel as if they can simply "change their minds" at will. Would be nice, wouldn't it, to be able to just "decide" to be confident and then have it be so? Fortunately there are practical things you can do to make a marked difference in the strength of your belief, and that's what this section of the book is all about.

The strategies to follow are a variety of *practical* things you can do to take some of the mystery out of building belief. Even if you don't think they'll make a difference, I guarantee that if you implement each strategy, you *will* increase your confidence and strengthen your ability to brave the obstacles and rise to the challenges that are a part of every endeavor worth pursuing. My belief is that if you can't change your mind, then change your behavior—eventually you'll reap the same rewards.

Belief Strategy #1: Affirmations

You probably have already heard about affirmations and perhaps already use them on a consistent basis. If so, good for you. I am convinced that affirmations are the foundation of our belief system, and I include this information as often as I can in everything that I teach. Regretfully, we live in a society full of negativity, which means we must make a conscious decision to feed our minds positive thoughts. I became acutely aware of the negative messages surrounding me when I decided that for one week I would not read anything negative in the newspaper. Guess what I found? I could read the entire paper in less than ten minutes. It almost boiled down to reading only the sales ads. We are consistently dumping so much negativity into our minds daily, weekly, that we are practically just garbage cans with hairy lids. My friend Bob Proctor, Life Success Productions, says it best: "Don't let anyone rent space in your mind."

What exactly is an affirmation? Webster's Dictionary defines the core word "affirm" as:

1. a: Validate, confirm
   b: To state positively
2. To assert as valid or confirmed
3. To express dedication to

Using this definition, you simply write a statement that confirms a positive optimistic outcome you see for yourself. Write the statement clearly, with detail and in the present tense, and read it ten times a day. This becomes the positive side of the debate that usually is going on in your head about whether or not you will succeed.

Did you know that you have 100 billion brain cells? The mind is so powerful that it can propel you toward success or hold you back with equal strength, depending on what you put into it. Garbage is always going in, and affirmations help you keep some of it away. I feel strongly that we allow our minds to mess with our potential. I use this statement a lot, and every time I say at a workshop, *"Don't let your mind mess with your potential,"* the room gets deadly silent. People immediately relate to what I am saying. They *know* how much negativity runs through their heads and that it affects them. Yet again, as strongly as the mind can influence us negatively it can also be so strongly positive that it can create health in the physical body. I watched John Kalench when he had pancreatic cancer—a disease that only two percent survive—over four-day spans go in for chemotherapy, get on a plane and go to a workshop, come home, go back for chemotherapy, then come into the office. I remember thinking, how in the world does this man do it? The answer was simple: with his mind. He was such an example of the power of attitude and expecting the best. Just being around him during that time strengthened me to believe in what the mind can do. I am sure you have seen people push through similar situations that would have easily caused most people to give up.

Combating the "garbage in, garbage out" of everyday life requires a conscious effort to take control. We have to take it upon ourselves to feed our minds positive, optimistic information. Yet the negativity that surrounds us—whether in the form of negative people or negative media—has a serious impact on our *perception* of potential. Our minds tell us we can't, and then we wonder why we struggle with believing in ourselves. The reason you can't is just because you told yourself you couldn't. We do it so naturally because it's the way the world is, and we don't even see it happening. Negative input begins at such an early age.

I conduct a prospecting workshop called "Prospecting Gems" and at every workshop, the students flow in and immediately say,

"Hi, Pat, I am so glad to be here today, I can't sponsor anyone, nobody wants to join, it's so hard, prospecting is just so difficult, and then I can't get them to stay in. . . ." These delightful new students arrive with all these "can'ts" and "won'ts." In one opening sentence, they've told me exactly how their minds are already messing with their potential.

The Power of Self-Talk

My friend Beverley Toney-Walter from my early days in this industry is an expert at helping people stop the constant flow of "can't" thoughts we all have with varying frequency. Here's how she explains the effect of negative thoughts, with a personal experience to illustrate it:

> The most direct and accurate indicator of your self-esteem is how you talk to yourself. It is those internal, often judgmental comments you make when you peek in the mirror or go about your daily life. Ponder the instances when you inspect yourself throughout the day. How many of these times do you compliment or congratulate yourself? Or, do you routinely criticize and compare? Positive or negative, your thoughts are powerful.
>
> You have inner voices talking to you constantly. One voice is your inner critic, and it can be the most damaging. Whether it sounds like Rambo or Mr. Rogers, this part of you can be quite vocal, judgmental, and vicious—if you let it. The critic compares you to others—a sibling or other family member, your best friend, or a movie star—with you on the losing end.
>
> Your critical voice sets impossible standards. It imitates and resembles a parent you could never please, even if you had walked on water or raised the dead. The critic reminds you of your failures and replays your most embarrassing moments in color, in 3D, in surround sound, the whole bit—just like in the movies (popcorn, anyone?)

Another one of the critic's unique and devastating talents is its ability to *chain* thoughts. Here is a personal example. Some years ago, a group of professors and teachers hired me to speak at a large university. During my talk, I mispronounced the word *hegemony*. A woman sprang to her feet from the audience and said vaingloriously, "If you are going to speak to professors, you need to learn how to pronounce words correctly." I thanked her and asked for the correct pronunciation, which she exalted in giving. Believe it or not, at the end of my seminar, I received a standing ovation.

Nevertheless, by the time I got to the airport to fly home, I could not recall the applause. The only thing I could remember was the woman's unkind criticism ringing in my ears. My critical voice grabbed this little juicy morsel and started chaining. "Way to go, Bev! What a disaster! You have no business speaking to professors! You might be articulating a lot of words incorrectly! What if it happens again? What if other people hear about this? What if that woman writes a letter to your boss and complains? You will lose your job!"

The good news is that this brutally destructive behavior can be stopped. Imagine that you are a magnet. Your center of attention attracts energy. When you concentrate on what you do not want, you literally magnetize that to you. The Law of Attraction cannot distinguish between what you *want* or *do not want*. It responds exclusively to the frequency you maintain. Whatever you sustain in thought, the Law of Attraction must match with people and circumstances. Make a choice immediately to dwell on *whom* and *what* you desire to become.

How do you transform your critical voice? Try this critical voice exercise. For one day, commit to staying conscious of your critical voice. (Expect your critic to become more vocal when you concentrate on it.) Write down verbatim what your voice vocalizes as it chatters to you. For example, if you hear, "You are so disorganized," you may be tempted to write, "You are messy." The first criticism is your critical voice. The second is your interpretation. Catch the critic in the act and document what it babbles, regardless of the message.

Often you will find your critic has a theme. Detect the theme. Once you recognize the theme weaving throughout your conversation, it is beneficial to give it a name. Naming the critic and identifying the theme seem to lessen their power.

For example, let us pretend that every time your critic voices its nasty opinion, it implies *you are not enough.* After analyzing a number of messages, you feel they are similar. You decide the critic is labeling you as *not enough.* This is your theme. Then you can more easily catch it in *the act.* Before, you were comfortable with hearing this ugly voice and did not notice the critic was programming you for failure. Now, catch the critic in action. This helps transform the critic into a supportive voice.

Excerpted from: *Mirror, Mirror on the Wall . . .*
Who is in there after all? by Beverley Toney-Walter

Until you can begin to question the negative assumptions that are guiding your thoughts and start exchanging them for their positive opposites, success will be an uphill challenge. I like the way Ralph Waldo Emerson spoke of this when he said, "Most of the shadows of this life are caused by standing in one's own sunshine." Interrogate your shadows.

Affirmations are one of the best tools available to you for tipping your mind's scale from negative to positive. I suspect you may have heard a lot about this—it's certainly nothing new, but *are you using it?* If you're one of the many who have put this valuable information on the back burner, but you are not seeing the results you want in your business, you need to make a new decision about it. Also, are all the new downline members you share your business with creating and saying their affirmations daily? Take responsibility for sharing this skill with them—you'll all be glad you did.

Remember to create your affirmations in the present tense— you have to be in the *now.* Say, "I am," not "I will be." This is what you are going to read to yourself every single day, so write them as if what you intend is already happening. You may even want to tape yourself speaking your intention and play it back on a tape recorder. To successfully shift your mind away from negativity, you must listen to or read your affirmations every day a minimum of ten times a day. This may seem like a lot, but the fact that people aren't usually willing to do it is exactly why those same people think affirmations don't work.

It doesn't happen automatically, it's not magic, it's the same activity as changing a habit. Just as it takes 21 days to create a new habit, if you don't change the mental habit of negativity by affirming the positive for a long enough time, of course your life won't change or be any different.

The Power of an Effective Affirmation

I remember hearing John Fogg read his personal intention on the *Build Your Vision* tape series. He read it so well and with such conviction that I forgot it was an affirmation and believed it was already true. It was as if he was just telling me what was so, and I thought, "I didn't know he had a house in Hawaii." Pretty soon, of course, I realized and felt silly, but he read it so well that I believed what he was saying was already fact.

If you had belief that clear and that convincing that someone else would believe it was so, can you imagine the effect of reading that to yourself every day? Can you see what a difference it could make in your life?

Affirmations give you an effective way of preventing your mind from messing with your potential—it's that simple. To whatever extent you have negative chatter in the back of your head is the extent to which you need to incorporate affirmations into your life as resistance. If you do it, you'll find over time that your belief is stronger—you'll take more positive actions to make that affirmation become reality.

∽

The ancestor of every action is a thought.
—*Ralph Waldo Emerson*

Question:
What are my actions saying about the thoughts I think?

Affirmation:
I listen to my self-talk to weed out any internal sabotage.

∽

Belief Strategy #2: Produce a Movie

The next step after creating your affirmation is to think of it—your intended future—as your Success Movie. Once you are totally clear on what you intend to get out of your business *now*—so much that you can close your eyes and see it—you're ready to make your "movie." You're the writer, the director, the producer, and most of all you will *star* in it. You decide whether it's going to be a short feature, a standard-length movie, or a full-blown epic.

Make it vivid, so that you can close your eyes and take yourself where you want to be. You want to transform your goals into an experience you can return to in lonely Maytag moments on the way to achieving all the success you deserve. If it's a vacation with your family, you've got to be able to smell the ocean, feel the sun on your face and the breeze in your hair, and see the kids playing on the beach.

If you could write a movie of your life, how would you write it? Who would the characters in it be? What would they be doing? See yourself in 90 days, in a year, in five years. You need to get this so clear that it is like a film—a film ready to be played at any given and needed moment in your mind.

Maybe your movie will be of you going up on stage receiving an honor from your company. You want to hear the applause, feel the heat of the lights shining on the stage, feel the weight of the award in your hands. You have got to be so clear in defining it, in seeing it that when you have one of those brief yet lonely Maytag moments—when you doubt yourself or what you are doing—you can close your eyes and literally go to your own movie. Mentally take yourself to *your* Success Movie—grab a seat in the "front row" and watch it.

One of the most important script writing rules is to be sure to write a *new* movie. Bob Proctor says that many people are visiting old movies—they're watching reruns instead of writing the new movies of their lives. Old movies are fun to watch late at night on TV, but no reruns for your Success Movie—unless you are one of the fortunate ones who has Success Reruns to replay.

Motivation vs. Inspiration

I constantly have people ask me, "How do I stay motivated?" as well as the bigger question, "How do I motivate my downline?"

I answer them by explaining that I am convinced it is actually inspiration, not motivation, that keeps people focused on their goals. Let me clarify the difference. Inspiration is internal, it's what's in your heart. Motivation is like a shower—you take one today, but you need one tomorrow. It won't last. It can also be compared to being outside on a cold winter day—you are cold and you come inside to get warm. If you have a fireplace, you instantly will back up to that nice toasty heat coming from the warm fire. You feel the warmth, and it feels great. However, when you step away from the warm fire and return outside, you will get cold again. In the same way, motivation warms you and feels great—but when you leave the person or thing that is motivating you, it is comparable to going outside again. The fireplace is no longer there to warm you.

You need to learn how to have an internal thermostat that you control and can turn up when you need it and choose to. That is what I call inspiration—the internal thermostat. Once you are clear about where you want to go and what your life can and will look like, you will *own* that thermostat—you will have clear intention. It's not enough to bring you success, but it will be there to help you push through any doubts and obstacles that will be in your success journey. If you depend only on enthusiasm from outside forces to motivate you to build your business and never get the inside job done right, you will be forever needing that outside stimulation.

Is motivation important? Yes! Just keep it in perspective—people who don't have the internal inspiration and intention can spend thousands of dollars going to all types of seminars, but until they feel it independently, until that faith and belief lives inside of them, they'll always need it. At some point, you have to take it inside yourself, become inspired, so that you have a place to go within and can lead yourself. That is when the miracle of intention will be realized.

Your movie serves to assist you in this. Make your movie inspirational—make it represent what you're inspired to aspire to. This is you taking positive action to achieve your goals. It's you taking responsibility for building a belief safety net so that you will refuse to let anyone or anything take you off course.

Unfortunately, it will often be your friends and family who will bring on these moments by trying to "save you" from network marketing. Sometimes the challenges will come from people who love you the most. When you think about it, it really makes sense—they care the most about you, so if they don't understand network marketing, they're more than happy to volunteer advice.

I'm a huge proponent of enrolling family just as soon as possible (we'll discuss that in detail in a moment). Until they are on board, you may have to go beyond the family circle to build your self-belief. One of the best ways to increase your confidence is to talk to people who don't put a "sister" or "brother," "daughter" or "son," "husband" or "wife" hat on you. Remember, if you have experienced less than success in other things, family can be just so kind to remember those times and remind you of them when that's the last thing you need to hear. Many people build multi-million dollar downlines, earn a six-figure income and drive luxury cars from their network marketing efforts, and their family and some friends will *still* say, "When are you going to get a real job?"

One of the hardest things about this is that family and friends are the people we're accustomed to going to for advice, but if they don't understand network marketing, they're not the right people to give it. If I was ill, would I go to a person without medical training for advice on my illness? In the same way, why would I go for business advice to someone who has absolutely no information or experience in it? Everyone has an opinion, and it's the one thing everyone wants to give away. Get your advice from informed, experienced people on the topic you are asking about.

Sandra Tillinghast has been frustrated more than once at seeing downline members suffer through this. "Whatever little belief I'm helping them build, they lose thanks to friends or family. I told one woman recently, who had two friends dump on her, to try this approach with them: 'You know, I just went through a training yesterday with my National Vice President, and the training was on dream-stealers. I had no idea what that was, until she started talking about it, and now I realize that some of my best friends right now are dream-stealers for me in my business. I want you to know that I know you're worried about me and that you're concerned, but I need for you to believe in me and keep whatever negative thoughts you have to yourself.'

"I told her I know for a fact that this works if you focus consistently and guard your mind and your beliefs. When you decide this is going to happen, it does start happening, but you have to decide it with 100 percent conviction and work a plan."

If you face misunderstanding from family, or worse, active disrespect or criticism, try using third-party validation to educate them. They're probably just uneducated about network marketing. If that doesn't change their opinion, it's better just to smile at them and move on. You can tell them that you know they want the very best for you, and then go be with people who share your belief, who've had some success, and who can help strengthen your confidence. Watch your self-produced movie to offset the dream-stealers.

∾

No one can make you feel inferior without your consent.

—*Eleanor Roosevelt*

Question:
Am I letting the slings and arrows of life get me down?

Affirmation:
I constantly find ways to feel good about myself, my business and my business associates by focusing on what is right and good.

∾

Belief Strategy #3: Enrolling Family

Family can be your biggest challenge or your biggest support. Even though not everyone in my family understood network marketing, my sweet husband and our two children were completely enrolled in my business. If you have a significant other and aren't doing the business with them, take the time to explain what it's about and why you're doing it. Ask for support—you'll probably get it, and it will make such a difference (not to mention making the business more fun).

My husband, Ollie, has always been tremendously supportive of everything I do. In my network marketing career, his part included unpacking orders, making sure my car was clean and filled with gas, assisting with the house—supporting my efforts in a general way. He had his career, which was very time-consuming, but he respected and helped wherever he could in my business. He was more of a behind-the-scenes business partner, while I was the one up front. He is a well-read, very intelligent, quiet personality. I'll never forget when one time at a seminar, someone asked him, "Oh, what do you do in the business?" and he very confidently, proudly, and firmly stated, "I don't hinder Pat." I thought it was a great answer. He knew what I did best, and so he did all the things that he could to free me to do them. He was and still is "the wind beneath my wings." How did our relationship progress to this? I enrolled him early to understand the benefits to him and the family.

Now when I travel, he frequently comes with me and finds things to do while I am speaking. Then afterwards, we get to go do things together. It's just wonderful—it's how we have evolved with the business together.

In the early days of developing my business, I understood the importance of enrolling the support of my family. To help my children understand my new role and adjust to my being out at night giving presentations and spending time on the phone, I let them set goals that my business could fulfill for them. If my daughter wanted a new toy or my son wanted a new skateboard, I'd cut out pictures of those things. I would then place them next to the pictures of what I wanted, and put them all on the refrigerator or the wall. I wanted them to experience the benefits of what I was doing from the very beginning. One of those goals was an annual family trip. For 14 years we enjoyed an annual trip to Disney World at Christmas. My kids thought that Santa Claus and Mickey Mouse were cousins. It was Disney every Christmas, bought and paid for by my network marketing business. This was even more exciting to me because before network marketing, I had not been able to enjoy vacations like this. I had never even been on a plane. I had never stayed in fine hotels. So to be able to share travel with my family meant a lot to me. All year we would put pictures of Disney World up on the wall—it became a tradition. If I got a complaint about helping me with carrying things to the car or doing the dishes, I'd start singing, "M-I-C-K-E-Y M-O-U-S-E," and they'd say "Oh, okay," because I had enrolled them in the benefits that my home-based network marketing business was providing all of us.

Enrolling children is so important—many times I've heard mothers and fathers talk about feeling guilty if they're away from their kids at a meeting or giving a presentation, when if you just teach them and enroll them in their goals, they'll be excited. And isn't the success of your network marketing business in their best interest? Kids are smart enough to understand that. While the business isn't always as flexible as people sometimes wish, especially in the beginning, my kids always knew I was working for the benefit of the entire family.

As you start making money, it's easy for it to get sucked into necessities, like the bills and unexpected expenses, but try to save a certain amount for a family treat. Take advantage of your company's contests and bonus programs and make something special for your family be your incentive for winning. It's good for you, for them, and for your business as a whole.

Motivation That Goes Straight to the Heart

I can tell you from personal experience that enrolling your family can become an amazing source of motivation.

My company often gave diamond rings as incentive awards. Since I didn't have diamonds back then, that was very exciting to me. That was something I'd always wanted, but with all the expenses of raising a family, diamonds just never made it to the top of the shopping list. I remember one time in particular when the company announced it was going to award *someone* with a sapphire and diamond ring. My daughter, Laura, knew how much I wanted it, so she cut a picture of a ring out of a jewelry ad in the Sunday paper, put a little piece of cardboard underneath it, and made me a paper ring. She'd seen me put up pictures of Disney World, and then we would go to Disney World; she'd seen me put up a picture of something else that I was going to earn with the company and take it down after I achieved it; so she made me this little paper ring to help me earn the real thing. I have it to this day. I have the real ring, and I have hers. I treasure it because, to me, it showed that she was learning a lesson—she understood the concept of belief, vision, and the power of intention.

Another one of my goals along the way was to earn a new Lincoln—the first real luxury car I was ever to own. When I heard about this incentive, I told everybody about this Lincoln I was going to get.

Laura asked me, "Mama, are we *really* going to get a new Lincoln?"

I held my hand out with the ring I'd earned on it, the one she had made the paper ring for prior to the real one. With that reminder of belief, intention, and achievement, she went running to her dad, yelling, "Daddy! We're getting a new car!"

With that kind of belief from her, how could I have let her

down? Her faith in me was the strongest motivator I could ever have had.

Belief Strategy #4: Kodak Moments

Real images work wonders for increasing the power of your mental movie. Sometimes when someone is new, they don't have photos of themselves in successful roles. I always suggest getting a role of film and taking success photos, whether at the car dealership in front of your dream car or in front of a dream house in the neighborhood you'd like to live in. I always encourage people to grab a camera and set out to take the pictures of their dream cars, dream houses—start creating those mental pictures—clips of their movies. As I would encourage those in my organization to do this, most of the time they wouldn't have the courage or belief in themselves to follow through with these photo activities. It sounds great at a meeting, but as they go off on their own, it just sounds silly, and they lose the courage to do it. Doubts creep in to cloud their intention, and they begin to think, "Why go to the trouble? It's not worth it."

In my business I decided to accomplish two things at once—help the people in my organization build their self-belief and enroll their families. I called a local dealership and told the dealer that I had about 100 people I wanted to bring down to look at his automobiles that Monday night. I went on to explain that my company gave automobiles as rewards for top field performance. I asked if I could bring my distributors and their families so they could choose which cars they wanted to set for their goal. I let him know that I was one of the top people in my company and had already earned several automobiles myself. He naturally agreed—how often did he have 100 interested buyers into his dealership on a Monday night? I promoted the event with lots of enthusiasm and told my downline to bring cameras, significant others, spouses, and children along for a fun time.

When we arrived, the car dealership manager was so excited that he'd put out refreshments and punch and had all of his salesmen there, dressed up, ready to share all the auto benefits. It was just great—the dealership sold the dream, and I didn't pay anything! They were thrilled. The women were sitting in the cars, flipping open the makeup mirrors and checking all the features. The men were all bonding underneath the hoods as they talked cams and horsepower. The kids were sitting in the back seats jumping up and down, saying, "Mama, Mama, are we really going to get this car?"

It was a beautiful scene. The energy in the group was pure excitement and fun. Then we made sure that every family got together around the car of their choice for family photos. When each family went home, they had a picture of themselves with their dream car to put up on the wall as a reminder of what was going to be earned. I was always careful not to use the word "win," because it's not a lottery—it's earned through effort. The car would be a reward if the work was done; if the family gave support, the whole family could enjoy it.

Everyone had so much fun that we started doing it every month. Being together with other excited people can have such an impact—they see others just like them confident and happy, and it is contagious. Many of them had never had a brand new car, and the distributors all supported each other in their efforts. When they finally achieved it, they went to that dealership, so it paid off for everyone.

Belief Strategy #5: Market YOU

One of the best things you can do for your self-confidence as you are out talking to people is to look and act the part before you make the part, or as it's commonly said, "fake it 'til you make it." If you offer someone a chance to build a successful business with you and you don't look successful yourself, they'll see the discrepancy. I'm not suggesting you rack up credit card balances or make car payments you can't afford, but do the best with what you have and set high standards for yourself. Small things can make a difference in how you feel about yourself and how people perceive you.

When I didn't have much money to purchase an extensive wardrobe, I would go to the better stores like Saks Fifth Avenue. Even though I couldn't afford any of their merchandise, I would try on the clothes, feel the best fabrics, and find out what made me look my best. Then I would go to the discount stores where they sold designer items at a reduced cost. I was able to recognize the best fabrics, the designer names and styles, and the cuts that looked the best on me. Like radar, as soon as I walked in the door, I would know what to look for. It enabled me to look like an attractive and competent business partner—I was determined to look the part. To this day I can go into a discount store and can spot the $500 jacket that is marked down to $79. Even though I can now afford full price, it is still fun to find a bargain.

Many people think you don't need to dress a certain way in this business, but I believe you really do. How you look and feel about yourself is a big part of your belief building. It also contributes to the belief that others will have in you. Their belief will build your belief. When you meet someone you only have seven seconds to make that first impression. If that impression is not the one you want to project, it may take a long time to change it.

I've always taught and believed that the same principle applies to your car. Even if you don't have the most expensive or stylish automobile, make sure the one you have is clean, polished, and tidy inside—no fast food wrappers on the floor. Does your car look like you live in it? Do you feel like you live in it? How proud do you feel when you open your car door? If you were to pick me up to go to a meeting, telling me about this wonderful lifestyle I can have in network marketing, and I get in your car and it looks like you live there, what am I going to think? How many times do you say when someone gets in your car, "Excuse the mess, it's not usually like this, but . . ." (you know the rest!)

If you are saying it more and more, *stop*—reevaluate the truth. If it derides your credibility, start cleaning your car on a regular basis. It will increase your pride, your self-belief, and you won't need to worry about the worn-out excuse for why it's a mess. Lead by example, even in the early days when *you* may be all that you are leading. You want to present yourself in such a way that others are inspired to emulate you—*duplicate* you. It's much harder to sell a dream you don't reflect. Polish your shoes; have at least one good outfit. Who cares if you wear it all the time? When you look better, you feel better, and you present yourself as a more appealing and self-assured potential partner for a business that depends on effective partnership. Whether you like it or not, you have to sell yourself before you can sell anything else. If *you're* not sold on yourself, creating a sharper image for yourself will serve both causes. Would you want to be sponsored by you? Make whatever adjustments necessary to be able to answer resoundingly, "Yes!"

Learning By Doing

When I did my first party, I sold approximately $500 of products, booked three more parties, and one guest actually wanted to sign up. I had no idea what I was doing, but I was excited. There I was, the new bumblebee, flying because I didn't know I couldn't, with this guest interested in the business. I did have enough sense to make an appointment with her, and I ended up sponsoring her— her name was Renee. She asked me, "How long have you been in the business?" and I said, "Oh, a while." The truth was, I'd been in about a week, but I was afraid she wouldn't believe in me, so I fudged the details.

Every time Renee called me with a question, I'd say, "Oh, Renee, I am so glad you called. I was just on my way out the door, and that's a great question. Let me jot it down, and as soon as I get back, I will call you."

Well, what I really had to do was run to my manual, because it was the blind leading the blind. My girlfriend was brand new when she sponsored me, so she didn't know very much yet. Our upline was so busy, she could never get back to me fast enough. When I finally had the answer, I would call Renee back and tell her what I'd found through research.

When I got my first company car five months later, some of the top people threw a little party for me, and everyone kept coming up to me saying, "Gee, Pat, you have done so great, and you've only been in the company this small amount of time!" Renee heard this and said, "Wait a minute, you have only been in five months? I've only been in for five months!"

"Yes, Renee," I admitted. "Actually, you were my first recruit and that was my first party. I didn't want to tell you because I thought you wouldn't want to be led by another newcomer." She couldn't believe it. She said I'd always seemed like I knew what I was doing.

And truthfully, that was my intention—I wanted her to be sponsored by a great leader. I wanted to be successful so much that I acted like I already was. I wanted her to believe in me. Honesty is the best policy, so I don't necessarily recommend this tactic, but you can see from this example just how powerful conscious self-presentation can be. I didn't want to tell her, "You know, I'm as green as you, girl, I don't have a clue." She told me that in fact, she would have been fine with it if I had, but it really had more to do with me than with her.

The bottom line was that I didn't have enough confidence in myself, so I wanted her to have it. I wanted to be the kind of leader I thought she would want to be sponsored by and became it along the way. I wanted to walk tall while I was learning.

Belief Strategy #6: Be Part of a Team

As soon as possible, align yourself with other people who share a similar vision. Hopefully you have been sponsored into an already existing team of visionaries. If not, create one as soon as possible.

Remember when I talked about tipping the mind's scale from

negative to positive? This is why being part of a team is so important, especially for part-time networkers. One of the great things about network marketing is that you're in business for yourself, but the flip side of that advantage is that sometimes you can feel isolated, like you're in business by yourself. If you're part of a team that gets together in person or over the phone on a regular basis, you have a support system that will help you keep your belief high.

It's important to immerse yourself in the community and activity of a team when you're first starting—more so than any other time in your business because you don't have the belief in yourself yet that you'll have once you've experienced some success. As a beginner, it can feel like you are walking on a tightrope over a deep cliff—without a safety net. When the journey gets shaky and rocky, it's extremely tempting to turn back. When you are surrounded by a team, though, it's like having a safety net underneath you. They will catch you if you fall and help you back up. The team can reassure you, affirm your decision, cheer you on, give you added belief in yourself. Even if I'm not a really great ball player, if I am part of a winning team, I am a winner by association.

As part of a team, you start getting recognition right away. In network marketing, recognition usually comes in the form of a check, but in the period before checks start coming in, a team can offer recognition through acknowledgment and appreciation. If you try to do the business in a vacuum, a few too many questions or doubts from outside forces can easily extinguish the flame of inspiration and excitement. A team is a safe haven for that flame and will help you to celebrate small victories.

In my workshops, I frequently ask the following questions I learned from Brian Biro, who I affectionately refer to as "my friend Mr. Team":

What's the greatest team you have ever been a part of?
What did you get from it?
What did you bring to it?

Every time I ask these questions, people yell out the most wonderful adjectives—*belonging, camaraderie, support, happiness, fellowship*—you couldn't go to a thesaurus and get any more beautiful human words. It's just amazing. I ask them to tell me some of the teams they've been involved in, and of course the most common ones mentioned are church, sports, and work. Some people say marriage, family. Never do I hear a single negative comment about teams. Being part of a team is one of the best physical, mental, and emotional supports that most of us have ever felt.

Finally, I ask:

If you could apply those team results to your network marketing business, what do you think you could accomplish?

Every time, the answer is: *Anything!* Learning to work on a team involves learning to find out who brings which good qualities and skills to the group. You have to grow and accept people where they are. Define each other's strengths and support each other in weaker areas so everyone achieves the goals. That's the synergy and the energy that comes together in effective teamwork.

～

Snowflakes are one of nature's most fragile things, but just look what they can do when they stick together.

—**Vesta M. Kelly**

Question:
Am I encouraging my business builders to be a community or just individual businesses?

Affirmation:
I remember that more can be accomplished as a team than as an individual.

～

Teams Make Us More

One of the best things about a team is that sometimes we're willing to be accountable to others when we won't be accountable to ourselves. So many people come into network marketing from a structured environment and experience difficulty adapting to the flexibility and freedom. You can hide when you aren't on a team. You can get up in the morning, you have nobody to report to, and you know that if you don't make your calls, you can sell yourself on whatever excuses you come up with.

A team can help fulfill the need for structure. If you have a team you meet with every Wednesday when you'll have to give a report on how you're progressing toward your goals, you don't want to show up each week with nothing to say. In addition, as you may know from personal experience, people will often do more for others than they will for themselves, and that's where the accountability comes in. Who likes to let a team down? Teams make you accountable, and in the end, it's still your business and you're still the one who will benefit from the rewards of your own accountability.

Brian Biro offers one of the best explanations I've heard of the effect teamwork has on individuals. In his book *The Joyful Spirit*, Brian refers to the Relay Paradigm, which has been the centerpiece of his work as a coach, teacher, and business consultant. In his years as a coach of the Junior Olympic swim team, he found that no matter what level of expertise a swimmer had attained, each was elevated to a higher level of performance when participating in relays. In his book *Beyond Success*, he describes the keys to becoming a master in the Relay Paradigm:

- **First** is developing absolute certainty that whatever your team needs, you'll deliver.
- **Second** is having a compelling purpose that's much bigger than yourself.
- **Third** is a natural outgrowth of the first two—once you're absolutely certain that you'll eagerly give everything you can to your team and committed yourself to a purpose that extends beyond yourself, you no longer fear competition. In fact, competitors become dynamic energy sources because they help you discover more of your true potential. You actually want them to excel, because you know their excellence will enable you to gain more energy and

concentration. In the Relay Paradigm, competition becomes the supreme form of cooperation.

A really good team will challenge each team member—the spirit is kind and generous, but they challenge nonetheless. If a team really cares about you, they will try to point you in new directions. Most of us just do things the way we always have without a thought, but when a team comes together, each person bringing a set of unique experiences, it may help you to see things in new and better ways. Maybe someone will introduce you to a more effective method of doing something or inspire you to try some new approach that makes your business explode.

And in the same way that you have to have an open mind to be coachable, you need an open mind to learn from your teammates and grow from the experience. Don't go in just expecting to benefit personally—listen to the other members and give of yourself.

CONCLUSION

What's in Your Gift Box?

What's in Your Gift Box?

Y ou slowly pull one end of the beautiful red satin bow so that it unravels gracefully around the corners of the elegantly wrapped gift before you. Blooming flowers in violet, gold, and blue decorate the crisp paper covering the top of the box as you lift it off to reveal the contents of this impressive gift. You look inside and see wonderful things that can all be yours if you simply reach in to claim them.

What do you see?

What are the gifts network marketing is offering you?

Isn't it time you accepted the gift?

I want to share with you here what one of our industry's strong leaders, Peggy Long, author of *On this Rock,* wrote to me recently. She said:

> "My dad, Dr. Kermit Long, a young 85-year-old minister, has a sermon that so touches me and others—it's about singing the song you were meant to sing.

*Inside us all there is a song that needs to be sung.
We were born to sing our song and make the world
complete.
Every song is different and cannot be replaced.
Do not wait too long to find your song and sing it.
What a tragedy to die, before we ever get to sing our
song."*

The question begs to be answered: If not now, *when?* Define what success means to you, make the choice to achieve that success in your life, and allow yourself to experience the miracle of intention. You don't have to know *how* it is going to happen, just that it *is* going to happen. If you truly intend it, the gift is yours! I wish you all that success means to you today and tomorrow.

About the Author

Pat Davis is a speaking professional with over 29 years experience in direct sales/network marketing. (She says she started in kindergarden!) Pat offers a three-dimensional experience rarely found in the network marketing industry/direct sales. She has "walked the talk" as field, corporate, and independent. After joining network marketing part-time to earn extra income as a young wife and mother, she embraced the opportunity and shared it with others. She grew to become one of her company's top leaders, top income earners and a multi-million-dollar producer. She went on to become the U.S. Vice President of Sales and Marketing for the same $300 million dollar international network marketing company.

Pat shared her expertise with tens of thousands when she served as CEO, speaker and trainer for Millionaires in Motion, Inc., an international independent training company. After over four years in this position, she formed her own company, Network Marketing Tutor, Inc. In addition to consulting, she facilitates workshops, keynote presentations, and specialty training for a myriad of network marketing companies and leaders.

Pat is not only recognized as a strong female role-model for this industry, but also as a highly qualified, seasoned master, true professional and polished presenter. She is uniquely qualified and excited to share her years of experience, knowledge, and passion for network marketing with others. Pat teaches and trains with the rare ability to relate to any audience in a fun, positive, and "down to earth" manner. She is known and respected for her client's results, making her a sought-after speaker and trainer internationally.

Also by Pat Davis

Prospecting Gems

Proven Techniques That Get Results! 4 audio tapes

Recorded live at the workshop that Pat Davis has delivered to audiences around the world. *Prospecting Gems* is a recruiting manifesto. Every year, millions of people join a network marketing company. Somebody's going to sign up the future stars, and if you'd like to find one or two for your own organization, *Prospecting Gems* will show you how.

Organized into 15 or 20-minute sections, each side of each tape is the perfect length. You'll learn how to present your business to different kinds of people. The "fear of prospecting" vanishes when you hear the section entitled "The Gift of Network Marketing," and you'll learn fun strategies that give guaranteed results.

Recipes For Successful Phoning

Book and Audio CD

Most networkers, regardless of experience, sometimes look at their telephone like it weighs a hundred pounds. Chances are, you've been there, too—stuck, seemingly unable to dial a number, while the clock ticked away your valuable time. This book and audio CD will guide you to get "un-stuck." Develop and fine-tune successful phone conversations for every situation.

Programs by Pat Davis

Prospecting Gems Workshop™

It is expected that within the next year alone, over eight million people will embrace network marketing to enjoy the financial and personal freedom that this great industry offers. How many of them will be in your organization? Prospecting is the lifeblood of your business. Use Pat Davis' acclaimed Prospecting Gems workshop and materials to tap into those eight million people. Sales leaders and network marketing companies alike use the Prospecting Gems workshop to enhance and diversify their training roster.

Women—The Spirit of Network Marketing™ Retreat

This woman's transformational retreat will help you to realize your full potential and unleash your inner power. You will learn the "nuts and bolts" of building a successful and prosperous business, woven beautifully with highly effective interpersonal skills. The retreat's program will enable you for success. You will leave equipped to create the life you have always known possible.

The WomensXchange™
A Mentoring Program by Women . . . For Women

The WomensXchange is just that—an opportunity for women to exchange ideas with other women. It's a forum in which to learn from other women, to take away something from each other's experiences and to discover how other women deal with certain issues. Finally an opportunity to belong to a program that allows you to examine how others have achieved success in their business and to network with other successful women. Visit—www.womensxchange.com

To request additional information on programs by Pat Davis
or any additional information on the materials or people
mentioned in this book, please contact:

Network Marketing Tutor, Inc.
7770 Regents Road #113-207
San Diego, California 92122
Toll Free Voice (888) 952-7000
Phone (858) 642-7546 • Fax (858) 587-2887
On the Web • www.networkmarketingtutor.com